CW00531226

The Sickle and the Crescent
Communists, Muslim League and India's Partition

The Sickle and the Crescent
Communists, Muslim League and India's Partition

Sunanda Sanyal & Soumya Basu

frontpage

frontpage

www.frontpagepublications.com

First published 2011

Frontpage Publications Limited
5 Percy Street, London W1T 1DG, United Kingdom

Frontpage
Level 6, Constantia
11 Dr U N Brahmachari Sarani, Kolkata 700017, India

ISBN: 978 81 908841 6 7

Printed in India
By Sadhana Press Private Limited
76 B B Ganguly Street, Kolkata 700012, India

Contents

Introduction

Of the two authors of this book, the first who hails from erstwhile East Bengal suffered the Partition (often called *vivisection*) while the second, born in West Bengal after the Independence, did not. The first, being in his middle teens in 1947, vividly remembers what happened in consequence of the Partition. The second's interest in the Partition is academic, but it makes him suffer even to this day, in a manner of speaking. The second, now being in his late twenties, did all the leg work – call it *research,* if you like. The product – the book – can hardly be called *history,* for the conclusions are not definitive.

We return to the upbringing of the authors. The first was brought up in Pabna, where his father, a doctor, set up a reasonable practice. Pabna was a quiet 'city' and his father was a Congressman – a *satyagrahi.* The doctor once a month led a team of volunteers, including a member of the Communist Party of India (CPI), all wearing goulashes, carrying a 'hazaak lantern' (a kerosene-lit contraption that gave a powerful light) to some nearby village on a literacy mission of sorts. The literacy rate before Independence was barely 6 per cent. Such were the times that the Congress and the CPI seemed to be fired by the same zeal for Independence. Such a conclusion may appear simplistic today, but at the top levels, probably, the Party leaders differed a little more widely than at the bottom. The politics of violence had not quite started yet, despite the riot in 1946. Vote banks were unheard of in those days.

Even so, the Partition became inevitable, following particularly the 'Great Calcutta Killing' on 16 August 1946. After the Independence, Pabna became part of East Pakistan. The doctor mentioned above planned to stay on in Pabna, thinking that a medical practitioner's job might be considered indispensable, or more probably thinking that the CPI's suggestion that the vivisection would not last might be correct. That was a widespread belief at that point of time. But one day 'something' happened – probably a patient refused to pay his fees – and the doctor decided to leave East Pakistan. Sometime in January 1949, he and his family set out for Iswardi, the nearest rail station, in a reserved coach, which stopped midway and the driver demanded an extra 30 rupees, which was a lot of money in those days. Again at Iswardi, as the family was clearing their household effects, including a phonograph, a police official came up to the doctor, and asked if he had obtained permission to "take all these goods to India". The doctor gave him a passive look, but said nothing.

Since no passports were required in those days, the family boarded a train to Ranaghat, for eventual travel to Chakdaha, a small village near to the border, where a so-called 'Pabna Colony' was coming up. Darshana was the last station in East Pakistan in their journey to India. The family waited with baited breath until that station arrived. When it did, all but their coach was thoroughly searched. As the train whistled past Darshana, we wondered if the doctor's golden silence had not done the trick. They thought it was good riddance, anyway. But life in India was not to be a flow of milk and honey. The doctor's family was spared, thanks to the reasonably good practice he was able set up again. But the endless stream of refugees that followed them soon suffered no end.

The first author had by then moved to Dum Dum, in the outskirts of Calcutta, having joined a college in Calcutta. One instance of the unending misery of the refugees will suffice. Sometime in February 1950, the Hindus in the Bagerhat subdivision of the Khulna district in the East Pakistan were attacked. Many of them crowded Khulna Station. This triggered a conflagration that could perhaps match the holocaust of the Great Calcutta Killing, which was, therefore, not the be-all and end-all. An NGO in Dum Dum took the first author and some young men to Ranaghat Station. The first author saw a number of trains, which could hardly be 'seen' because of the humans clinging to every inch of space, from East Pakistan trundling into Ranaghat. The platforms filled up minutely with refugees, who ran into two men 'with a revolver'. Nobody seemed to know who caught them. None even cared to ask if they were Hindu or Muslim. All that mattered was, "Why are they hanging around?"

The refugees pounced on them. They kicked and punched, and at least one of them must have bitten into raw flesh, for his teeth were bloodshot. Within minutes the two men were done to death, who, or which, throbbed like pounded flesh. Kalyan Datta, the frustrated Communist, who believed that the Congress and the Muslim League shared the blame equally for the Great Calcutta Killing, describes the fratricidal riot of 16 August in these words: "I'm not one of those who go lyrical over Calcutta's soft spot for revolution. Actually the student or the labourer who bares his chest before a bullet can also murder his classmate or colleague."

Swadhinata, the Bengali daily of the Communist Party, carried a report on the riot from Metiabruz, Calcutta says Kalyan Datta. It described how the Muslim workers searched the rooms and killed the fellow Oriya members of the same union. The Oriya members showed their red cards and begged for life, but to no avail. The riot occurred on 16 August 1946, and I went out in the afternoon of the following day. Trams and buses were off the road. There was no trace of the riot from Belgachia to Shyambazar. But as I walked down Cornwallis Street (now rechristened as Bidhan Sarani), I found some remnants of shops that had been gutted, and a number of dead bodies. But I will never forget what I saw at the main entrance to Hatibagan Bazar.

I saw a heap of dead bodies in *lungi* (i.e. Muslim), laid one upon another, on the side of a street. I heard later that these men, who ran around like rats in a trap, were prodded to death with lathi, rod and brickbat. Further ahead I found a rag-picker of 19 or 20 lying close to a litterbin. Her face was unruffled, as if she were sleeping peacefully. She was still clutching at her sari soaked in blood that had blackened. I thought no Muslims could attack Hatibagan Bazar. There was no question of disturbing the peace. Still how could so many people be bashed and prodded to death in cold blood? Death resulting from a clash between two groups people, I understand. But how can one think of men descending to the bestial level of beating to death helpless people?" (Translated from the Bengali).

At this distance in time, it is futile to blame the start of the riot on any particular community, much as the call for Direct Action may in the ultimate analysis be held responsible for it. Sandip Bandyopadhyay (*Itihaser Dike Fire: Chhecholliser Danga:* Turning an Eye on History: Riot of 1946), who gives a day by day account of what happened, may help one to reach one's conclusion. According to Bandyopadhyay, Md Usman, Mayor of Calcutta Corporation, announced the programme of Direct Action on 9 August 1946. He called upon the people (Muslims, that is) "to muster strong at the Maidan Meeting and make it a historic rally". He announced that, on 16 August, someone from the Muslim League would be present in every mosque.

On 11 August, the League announced: "It was in Ramzan that permission for jihad was granted by Allah. On 14 August, the members of the Muslim National Guard were called upon to assemble in Muslim Institute at 8.30 am." On 15 August, Nurul Huda, a leader of the League, having formed a so-called Muslim national core of railwaymen, said in his address: "No more slogans. The clarion call has come for action and nothing but action." On 16 August, an editorial article in the *Morning Star* addressed the Muslims in these words: "Mind you, 16 August, Friday, is the day of Direct Action, when we have to prove to the world that we are pledged to the creation of Pakistan." On top of this, Nazimuddin had already said, "We are not restricted to non-violence".

Sukharanjan Sengupta gives a graphic description of what triggered off the refugee influx in 1950 [Sengupta, Sukharanjan, *Bango Sanhar Ebong* (in Bengali)]. What follows is based on his account of the riot in 1950. According to Sengupta, the Muslims in East Bengal never quite thought of getting rid of the Hindu population. The local government still employed some 25 to 28 per cent Hindus. Some 50 per cent Hindus manned non-government organisations like educational institutions, health services, courts etc. In fact, it was impossible for Muslims to fill in the vacancies if all Hindus quit. Indeed, the eventual spread of riot to 12 districts on 10 February 1950 was altogether unexpected. Actually, it spread from some 35 lakh Hindus (in East Pakistan) to West Bengal – Tripura, the Brahmaputra valley and Cachar of Assam. The retaliatory riot put the Muslims in West Bengal at risk in the districts adjacent to the industrialised parts of the state. Not even the Partition could affect Bengali society so much as this riot of 1950. A new generation of youngsters were born in the railway stations, coaches, shanties, and in lands forcibly occupied. This upset the value-systems of numerous Bengali families.

Jawaharlal Nehru once commented: "The Partition of the country brought many evils in its train." The platforms of Sealdah Station, where numerous families sheltered, were a veritable mess. A UPI report, published in Amrita Bazar Patrika on 20 October 1948 said:

More than 1,000 refugees are now stranded at Sealdah Station making the South and Main station platforms their temporary abode. West Bengal Government vans visit the station every day and remove about 300 refugees daily but fresh batches come in and fill the vacuum. The platforms are packed with refugees presenting a serious problem to the passengers. With their small belongings here and there and shabby beddings spread all around, the sanitation condition of the station has been made horrible. Cases of cholera, influenza and dysentery have already taken place and there have been half-a-dozen cholera deaths during this week.

Whereas the middle class Hindus have taxed their friends and relatives in Calcutta and suburbs by sharing their overcrowded homes, the lower middle class, peasants, small village artisans, day labourers and petty shopkeepers have occupied the platforms awaiting their removal to government camps. They are a cross section of people – weaver, fishermen, artisans, clay-makers and others. They have come with their small belongings – a few with their instruments – and they want to settle down in West Bengal's rural life and pursue their vocation in this part of the Indian Dominion.

What added to the massiveness of the influx was a failing economy. The report continues:

The head of a family of four consisting of three young women and a baby-in-arms belonging to a village in Barisal related that while crimes like dacoities and robberies had considerably increased in villages, police protection was almost negligible. Most Hindu families of the village had already left. Mounting prices of rice, oil and other daily necessities of life and fear of assault on women hastened their departure.

Another man from a village in Chandpur recounted that 'paddy riots' had started in this village and surrounding areas. The paddy grown in his fields was forcibly taken away and nothing was left on which he could depend.

A man from Noakhali reported, 95 per cent of the Hindu families had already left. He stayed on but found it extremely difficult to eke out a living. He was a priest but sometimes also did manual work. He and his family were starving but nobody took any notice of them. Government help was also not forthcoming. So he made for Calcutta. On the way, he found hundreds of others moving in the same direction. They had the same sad story to tell: difficult condition of living and hatred of the Muslims. He gathered from his fellow travellers that famine conditions were prevailing in the interior of East Bengal. But if famine conditions prevailed there, how could the Muslims stay on? Muslims did not leave, he reported, because they were receiving relief from the State. The *Patrika* reporter found the adult member of a family groaning with high temperature. But he could not go to the hospital as he did not know what would happen to his young wife and three children if he went to the hospital.

Would you believe this riot was sparked off by a rumour at Barisal that the Hindus in Calcutta had murdered Fazlul Huq in Calcutta? Actually the Huq sahib had come to Calcutta to sell off his house on Jhowtala Road, near Park Circus. The West Bengal Government provided him with a car and security guards. Some seven thousand Hindus were murdered in one go. Not a single Hindu was left alive at Saestabad, some distance by steamer from Barisal. Postponing the sale of his house in Calcutta, the Huq sahib dashed back to Barisal and held, in and around that city, some 16 meetings, where he said: "Look, I am not dead. Do you realise the enormity of what you've done?" As the riot raged in Dhaka, Barisal and numerous other districts of East Pakistan, a retaliatory riot started in West Bengal. Some 90 per cent of the workers of the jute mills in 24 Parganas, Howrah and Hooghly were from Bihar, of whom about 70 per cent were Muslims. Very many of them were killed. One incident needs to be retold.

The Andrew Yule Company, founded by George Yule, owned a big mill in 24 Parganas. George Yule was one of the founders of the Indian National Congress. In fact, he presided over the Allahabad session of the Congress in 1888. George's grandson, A L Cameroon was President of the nation's oldest chamber of commerce named Bengal Chamber of Commerce. He happened to be there Chief Proprietor and the largest shareholder of the company owned by his grandfather. At that point of time, Ram Chatterjee, who was regarded as a top leader of West Bengal Socialist Party, and a faithful follower of subsequent Marichjhanpi fame, perpetrated by Jyoti Basu, was the main attacker of Muslim slums around the mills. The attackers were repulsed a number of times by the security guards of the British owner.

Cameroon complained to the authorities for not doing enough to protect his Muslim workers. He even sheltered the slum dwellers in the offices and factories. Cameroon thus became the target of the rioters. At the height of the riot, he set out in a car, driven by a Muslim driver, to find out how safe his workers were. After he had inspected some of the jute mill areas, his car stopped at a level crossing. The rioters surrounded his car and murdered his Muslim driver first and then himself. The gruesome incident happened on 26 March 1950. Prime Minister Jawaharlal Nehru and Maulana Abul Kalam Azad rushed to Calcutta, and because the District Magistrate of Howrah, Adhikram Majumdar, had failed to arrest Ram Chatterjee, the Maulana called him *betamij* (i.e. "scoundrel"), and was soon transferred.

Be that as it may, there were also examples of courage and humanism. "I witnessed an instance myself. One day, as I was travelling in a tram car, I saw a crowd around a man in *lungi* on Sealdah Station. It was clear what was going to happen. The conductor rang the bell, stopped the car and got off. He elbowed in and dragged the man out, got on the tram together with him, and sped off. Not a word was spent, nor was there any excitement, the conductor looked as if a minor roadblock had been cleared. The tramcar union could tell many such glorious stories of anti-communalism. The credit for this goes to the communist leadership of the union. Somnath Lahiri, Mohd Ismail, Ketanarayan Misir, Dhiren Mazumdar spent days and nights in the tramwaymen's digs and educated them politically. The Communists' role in anti-communalism is glorious. Even then, they could not prevent communal riots. Not even leaders like Gandhi and Nehru succeeded" (Translated from *Amar Communist Jiban* by Kalyan Datta).

On 8 March 1950, Nehru, accompanied by Shymaprasad Mukherjee and Dr Bidhanchandra Roy on the one hand, and Indira Gandhi and Congress leader Mridula Sarabhai on the other, spent hours in a number of refugee camps on Jessore Road around Bongaon Station, which was close to the East Pakistan border. Jawaharlal returned to Delhi on the following day, and on 10 March, he wrote to Nawabzada (that is, Liaquat Ali Khan), among other things:

I returned from Calcutta last night after four days' stay there...As more and more facts came to my knowledge and the effect that those facts and occurrences had produced on people's minds, I was greatly depressed . . . I had suggested to you that you and I should visit East and West Bengal . . . My sole object was to help in soothing people and in bringing back some normality. You did not agree to this proposal for the reasons you gave and thought that it would not do any good.

I still think that a joint tour of ours would produce a very great impression both in East and West Bengal.

I am so anxious to do something in my individual capacity that I have been thinking repeatedly of visiting some of these places, not as Prime Minister but as a private individual. It is just possible that my visit might shake people up. I attach so much importance to this that I would gladly give up my Prime Ministership and go to East and West Bengal entirely as a private citizen and stay for a while there. I would not do so with the object of carrying on an enquiry and of casting blame, but just to give some heart and confidence to the people I meet, whether Hindus or Muslims. I think I have some capacity to do so. I wish you would agree to my doing so, that is my going to Pakistan as a private individual for a stay of a few weeks" (Sengupta, Sukharanjan, *Bango Sanhar Ebong*).

Dr Roy welcomed the exchange of visits between the two Prime Ministers, when Jawaharlal wrote back to Dr Roy that "in the course of the letter (to Liaquat Ali) I mentioned that I had been approached by Basanti Devi and that she had expressed a desire to go to Dacca" (*Ibid*).

Jawaharlal was quite concerned about the Muslims who wanted to leave for East Pakistan. He wrote to Dr Roy:

16 March 1950
My dear Bidhan,

The Pakistani press contains references to harassment and ill-treatment of Muslims at Sealdah Station. I enquired about this from some people who came to see me both Hindus and Muslims. Independently they told me this was so and indeed that there was some danger of stabbing of Muslims there.

Amtus Salam, who used to be with Gandhiji, has come back from Dacca. She tells me that some women, whom she met there (one of these used to go to Gandhiji) also complained of a great deal of harassment at Sealdah Station when she was leaving Calcutta some days ago. This woman has written rather a pathetic letter to me saying that it has broken her heart to have to leave India which was her home, but conditions became impossible for her to stay on here.

I hope you will issue directions for the proper treatment and protection of Muslims at Sealdah Station. This is just what we are claiming from Pakistan and we cannot behave otherwise ourselves.

It is clear that Muslims in Calcutta are in a state of extreme panic. Their departure in large numbers is sufficient proof of this.

I am informed the Hindus are taking forcible possession of many Muslim houses so as to get the Muslim into trouble.

I gave a note to Amal Home today to be shown to some newspaper editors. I asked him to give you a copy. I feel that Calcutta papers are responsible for a great deal of mischief and this must be brought home to them. They are playing very irresponsibly with fire.

Among the worst papers the RSS Swastika, Jugantar, Basumati and Amrita Bazar Patrika.

The Azad paper of Dacca is coming here and doing g good deal of mischief. Amtus Salam suggested that separate compartments might be provided for Muslims going away from Calcutta by train. This is what the Pakistan people are doing for the Hindus coming here. This will afford protection to them.

The Peace Committee people came to see me today, among other things, asked for help from the police in order to trace lost people. I understand some people have a tendency to separated from their families and get lost. This apparently applies to Muslims especially in the circumstances.

Amtus Salam told me that the East Bengal Government had something (not much) towards rehabilitating Hindus. They had given some money to each family and sent to back to their old homes. This had produced some impression. She suggested that a beginning might be made towards rehabilitating the Muslims here who had fled from their houses or whose houses were destroyed. I understand that a very large number of houses were destroyed in Maniktala etc.

Among the Muslim houses raids by local Hindus and East Bengal refugees is said to be House No. 2 Chakku Khansama Lane, Amherst Street. It is reported that the inmates were forcibly driven out and their belongings were thrown out.

According to both French and other reports, Ram Chatterjee and Shashi are notorious gangsters of Chandernagore. The French say they have committed a good few murders. Apparently they were partly responsible for the trouble in Chandernagore and roundabout I am told that they have been appointed as relief workers for Muslim refugees in Chandernagore and are securing certificates of good character from the Muslims.

I am mentioning this as it has been decided to make a further change in the administration of Chandernagore.

You remember that the merchants who came to see me were very anxious that their Muslim workers should go to the factories. Some have apparently gone back, but on the other hand, I understand that there is a tendency to push them away to Pakistan by train. If they go away, our production will suffer.

Individual stabbings appear to continue in and round about Calcutta. It is difficult to deal with this kind of things. Nevertheless, this has a very bad effect both in India and Pakistan. On the whole, East Bengal appears to be, for the moment, free from such incidents.

The Hindu Mahasabha and RSS propaganda both for war and for a Hindu State has a very bad effect in the present tense situation. I wonder if this can be discouraged.

Yours,
Jawaharlal

The cumulative effect of the riots, consequent on the Partition, triggered numerous problems, of which the refugee influx was the most crucial one. Where did they live? Just anywhere – in the camps and on the platforms of Sealdah Station, for example. We will record here two reports, both taken from Prafulla K Chakrabarti's *The Marginal Men: The Refugees and the Left Political Syndrome in West Bengal*, which is generally regarded as a faithful account. The first one is by Jatin Saha, an inmate of the Ultadanga Relief Camp: "I reached the camp in the night and found a space marked out for me in a room in the first floor. When in the morning I tried to make my way to one of the four latrines for 1,000 people in the camp, I found that I could not reach the latrine without literally wading through a thick layer of human faeces. Besides I found that the entire courtyard and solitary tube-well were smeared with faces."

The other one represents the UCRC's (United Central Rehabilitation Council) experience. The UCRC team included Bijoy Mazumdar, Ambika Chakrabarty (of Chittagong Armoury Raid fame), Dr Naresh Banerjee and two others. Bijoy Mazumdar's story is said to be "corroborated by numerous eye-witness accounts of the Cooper's Camp and Dhubulia Camp". The team entered a large room and found some dozen corpses stacked against the wall, all bloated and stinking, while the women chatted away, the children played, and the men, pulling long faces, talked about grim the future ahead. The *Swadhinata,* the mouthpiece of the Communist Party of India, carried the picture of the corpses next day. But the paper never asked who made it possible for them to be killed?

We have already said what follows is not history. It is actually a question: who is responsible for the untold sufferings of the millions of our fellow countrymen? Be that as it may, most of the documents quoted here are from the newspapers published all over India, and the police archives. It is our hope that these documents will help the reader on to his own conclusion – or at least generate an interest in him to find out.

Sunanda Sanyal
Soumya Basu

26 January 2011

CHAPTER ONE

Puran Chand or P C

From the very outset, the Communist Party of India, a section of the Communist International, has been externally controlled and directed. That, in our view, is its biggest drawback. To begin with, it was under the spell of the Moscow based Communist International or Comintern. However, during the second decade of the bygone century, M N Roy, the erstwhile National Revolutionary-turned-Communist, along with his other Indian counterparts in exile, formed a Communist Party of India at Tashkent.

Later, Roy's expulsion in December 1929 brought the Party directly under the control of the Communist Party of Great Britain or CPGB. Further, men like Rajani Palme-Dutt, Ben Bradley and Harry Pollitt started calling the shots. Thus, the Indian workers had to follow the dictates of their British comrades who had little practical knowledge of the Indian situation. For example, when the entire nation stood by the Congress against the Imperialist oppression during the heyday of Civil Disobedience Movement, the Communists were missing. The CPI, following the International Line, was distancing itself from the National Bourgeoisie, which was the then policy of the Comintern. In fact, they started a League against Gandhism, with the slogan, "Anti-Gandhism is anti-Imperialism". The Party was banned once the Salt Movement had subsided.

Early Indian Communists were a scattered bunch with the exception of Bengal, Bombay and certain other pockets remaining active. Small Communist groups were formed in Bengal (led by Muzaffar Ahmed), Bombay (led by S A Dange), Madras (led by Singaravelu Chettiar), United Provinces (led by Shaukat Usmani) and Punjab (led by Ghulam Hussain). Later, in the thirties, the name of Puran Chand Joshi was added to this list.

Puran Chand, or just P C Joshi, was born on 14 April 1907 at Almora in the UP. His father, Pandit Hari Nandan Joshi, an educationist, rose to the level of Director of Education in the princely state of Rewa, Central Provinces. His son, too following in the footsteps of his father, passed his Matric from Government High School, Hapur (Meerut district), Intermediate from Almora's Government Intermediate College, with a gold medal in Sanskrit. Puran completed his MA in 1928 and LLB the next year from Allahabad University. A distinguished scholarly background started from a dingy little School room in the Hills teaching Sanskrit or some other subject, but destiny led him to achieve greatness in life.

In 1926 as a college student Puran was attracted to Pandit Motilal Nehru's brand of Swarajya Politics, and joined the Allahabad branch of Nawjavan Bharat Sabha. Later, he became a member of Allahabad Youth League, with Jawaharlal Nehru as President. The transition from such volunteer groups to the main Nationalist Organisation seemed obvious. But one particular Congress Session moved Puran's heart and soul.

During the Congress session held in Calcutta in 1928, the small town studious Congress volunteer Puran Chand met Aftab Ali, the labour leader. It was from him that Puran got smuggled copies of Palme-Dutt's "Modern India" and M N Roy's, "Future of Indian Politics". These two treatises introduced Puran to the theory of Marxism. Thus began the journey of an Indian Communist, who would be instrumental in building up a truly mass based, well-organised Communist Party in India.

That very year, Joshi's Communist career commenced with being the Secretary of the Workers' & Peasants' Party at its Meerut session in

September. This was followed by the membership of the Communist Party next year. Joshi, then just 22, found himself in the company of a group of political workers, who like others, wanted India's emancipation, but believed in the gospel of class-antagonism. According to them, real freedom would be achieved only after the establishment of a Proletarian-Raj. There was no point in selecting Macaulay's children in place of 'Pucca' sahibs. Puran understandably was attracted to the Marxist point of view, which, at least in theory, was tinged with Humanism.

In late 1920s, the Government was not just sitting idle. In 1929, all the comrades who had some kind of standing were rounded up and put behind bars. The charge was sedition; the case in question being the Meerut Conspiracy. The principal protagonist was one M N Roy, but he had absconded. This case created sensation at the time, claiming aggressive media coverage. The Communists replied against the charges from the dock. The case turned out to be a boon in disguise, as it provided a widely covered propaganda of Communist ideology at the Government's expenses!

Joshi was sentenced six years in the penal settlement of the Andaman Islands. Considering his age, the punishment was later reduced to three. After his release in 1933, Joshi worked towards bringing a number of groups under the banner of the Communist Party of India (CPI), only to be re-arrested the next year in connection with the Muir Mill Strike at Kanpur.

Meanwhile, the Comintern in its 7th Congress, 1935, formulated the United Front Policy for the colonies. Thus in such colonies the Communist Parties were advised to rally round the principal anti-imperialist National Bourgeoisie force (in case of India it was the Congress). By then Roy had been branded a renegade and expelled. The Party, in India, being illegal had to be re-organised and worked under the cover of another grouping. It had to quickly become a mass-based party in order to emerge as a decisive force in the political arena. A leader who could inspire became an overriding necessity. Towards the end of 1935, Joshi became the new General Secretary and the decision is believed to have been made under the influence of Palme-Dutt. Senior leaders like Dange, Adhikari or Mujaffar were overlooked. Hence in 1936, at the age of 28, Puran Chand Joshi became the General Secretary of the Communist Party and remained the brightest star in the Communist firmament.

When in 1949, Joshi was castigated, criticised and ultimately expelled from the Party on the charge of being a reformist by B T Ranadive and several others, his erstwhile comrades forgot the services he had rendered. In reality, the plans PC formulated turned out to be immensely beneficial for the growth and general well-being of the Party.

Joshi took two steps. Firstly, as the Party was banned, it started working under the guise of the so-called National Front. Keeping the International Line in mind, this National Front joined the Congress at its Lucknow Session in 1936. They were lucky as the man presiding was Jawaharlal Nehru, a self-professed Socialist. Among the Leftist groups within the Congress, the influential one was the Congress Socialist Party or CSP with firebrands such as Jai Prakash Narayan, Achyut Patwardhan, Ram Manohar Lohia, Minoo Masani, Ashok Mehta, Yusuf Mehrally and others. Likewise, M N Roy with his League of Radical Congressmen had also found a foothold on the Congress platform. Above all, Nehru and Subhas Chandra Bose were among the leaders.

This was not all. In the thirties, especially in Bengal, around a dozen Left Parties existed with almost everybody claiming to be the 'original' messiah of the down-trodden. These were (alphabetically arranged):

- Abhaya Ashrama Group
- Bengal Kirti Kishan Party
- Bengal Labour Party (Niharendu Dutta Mazumdar)
- Communist League of India (Soumyendranath Tagore)
- Indian Proletarian Revolutionary Party or Gananayak Party
- Jessore-Khulna Yuva Sangha
- Karakaan Party
- Lal Nishan Party
- Samyaraj Party

- The Revolutionary Party of Indian Working Class
- The Socialist Party

In addition, two other strong contenders, Revolutionary Socialist Party of India (or RSPI) and the Forward Bloc, came into existence by 1939-40. To prove oneself to be the 'official' representative of the 3rd International amidst such esteem company was a daunting task. Undoubtedly, the biggest road-block seemed to be the CSP. Joshi's plan was simple: enter CSP and take it over.

At the 3rd CSP congress, held in Faizpur, several communists were included into the CSP National Executive Committee. Two communist, E M S Namboodiripad and Z A Ahmed, became All India joint secretaries of the CSP. The CPI also had two other members inside the CSP executive. On the occasion of the 1940 Ramgarh Congress Conference, the CPI released a declaration called Proletarian Path, which sought to hit out at the British Empire, much weakened by war, and gave a call for general strike, no-tax, no-rent and so on in preparation for an armed revolutionary uprising. The National Executive of the CSP assembled at Ramgarh took a decision that all communists would be expelled from CSP; by then the Communists had, however, gained in strength.

In reality, this was but a dress-rehearsal for the eventual take-over of the National Congress. Joshi's pet project was to infiltrate into an organisation – and then capture it. He tried it with the AITUC and the Kishan Sabha and finally with the Muslim League. Joshi's other policy was unique: create a number of ancillary units and work in tandem with the Mother party. The purpose of such units would be to draw non-Communists to its fold.

Some of them (alphabetically arranged) were:
- All India Students' Federation
- Chatri Sangha
- Friends of Soviet Union
- Indian People's Theatre Association

- Kishore Bahini
- Mahila Atmaraksha Samiti
- Progressive Writers' Association

Joshi's stress on the cultural front yielded rich dividend. It was like the spider inviting the naïve fly into her parlour. A number of non-Communist cultural workers – novelists, painters, dramatists, musicians were easily attracted to these cultural groups. Later, when they became aware of the political purpose, some stayed back as the Marxist ideology had a certain romantic undertone. Exceptions were there, particularly in Bengal, for example, in case of Mahila Atmaraksha Samiti or MARS: Rani Mahalanobis, Leela Majumdar, Indira Devi Choudhrani (the first President of the MARS) left the organisation. On the other hand, the converts influenced a section of the society through their cultural activities. But, true, the Marxist ideology proved a great draw for the youth. No other political parties could offer such novelty.

In fact, both the Congress and the Muslim League emulated Joshi's plan later.

CHAPTER TWO

War and the People's War

The Second World War commenced on 1 September 1939, with the invasion of Poland by Nazi Germany – and subsequent declarations of War on Germany by most of the countries of the British Empire and Commonwealth and France. The Communist called it, following their International Line, an Imperialist War. The Nationalist forces launched a vigorous attack on the Colonisers. This was the time when a Non-Aggression Pact was in place between Russia and Germany, although the left block in the country, especially Subhas Chandra Bose, advocated a struggle against the British Government, with the Congress initially remaining undecided.

On 22 June 1941, Germany invaded the Soviet Union (Operation Barbarossa). Later, however, a change occurred in the theatre of war. Russia entered the Allied Formation with Great Britain and America. However, Communists world-wide seemed to be duty-bound to rally round their Fatherland. The nature of the war, at least to the Communist, changed. It became, not just anti-Imperialist, – but a People's War. Joshi had an explanation for the change in stance: "It is the People's War, because the peoples of the world have an incomparable leader in the USSR, which is demonstrating how a people's war is to be fought and won, and inspiring other peoples with indomitable courage . . . To doubt this is to be a cynic, lacking faith in one's own people, of the people of the whole world, and of course, the family of free peoples that is the USSR" (Our Policy: Joshi, P C, *People's War*, 5 July 1942).

The policy of the Communist towards Russia's principal allies, Britain and America changed along with the perception. The CPGB, which rallied in support of His Majesty's Government's war-effort, directed the Indian counterparts to follow suit. But the sudden somersault clashed with India's national interest. One can still ask how could Indians be allies of British Imperialism? Wouldn't it have been more appropriate for India to join the war only after she had been assured of her own freedom on its conclusion?

After all, to the common man, Imperial Britain, as much as Nazi Germany, was the enemy number one. True, there was a general sympathy for the Axis Powers among a large section of the people, but that was due to the anti-British feeling, throughout the nation, and understandably not due to any ideological affinity for Fascism (Roy, Dipti Kumar, *Leftist Politics in India*, p.196).

Not that the Communist were not worried. They were pondering over these facts. For at least six months, the anti-war attitude persisted amidst much debate and wrangling in the Deoli Detention Camp. There, some important Communists had been detained until a letter from Harry Pollitt, Secretary of the CPGB, ordered a clear switch-over. This letter is believed to have been delivered to the Communists in the detention camp – courtesy Sir Reginald Maxwell, the then Home Member of the Government of India. Rajani Palme-Dutt, too, in a letter to the Indian comrades, which was later published in *People's War* (English language organ of the Party) wrote, "By the time this reaches you, events will have moved much further and you may be in the midst of big issues ... The general line is clear, maximum mass mobilisation against Fascism, full co-operation in practical action with all who oppose fascism irrespective of political differences, no action of the present ruler so long as they stand by the alliance to resist Fascism, should deflect us from this line" (Masaani, Minoo, *The Communist Party of India*, p.80-82).

The Communists in Deoli – Dange, Mujaffar, Mirajkar, Ajoy Ghosh, Ranadive – had no choice but to agree to the new People's War theory of the International. The stance was clear: "The Communist Party in all countries were requested to recognise that Hitler's Fascism as the main enemy and the war waged by the USSR in alliance with Britain and America, as a war which had to be won by all people in the interest of defending the base of the world revolution. This duty and attitude were imposed, thanks to the internationalism of the Party. No national or local conditions could render it invalid" (Roy, Subodh (Ed.), *Communism in India: Unpublished Documents, 1939-45*, Vol. III, p.318). The People's War thesis was thus adopted at the Politburo meeting on 15 December 1941.

The Government at that point was looking for allies amongst Indian political parties e.g. the Muslim League, Hindu Mahasabha, M N Roy's Radical Democratic Party, the Unionists and Ambedhkarites. In course of a debate in the Legislative Assembly, Sir Reginald clarified the Government's position: "If there be any person whose attitude is such that he wishes earnestly to help the war effort, I have no desire whatsoever to keep him in Jail" (Overstreet/Windmiller, *Communism in India*, p.206).

The Communists in the detention camps, as well as those who were at large, conveyed to the Government that they were willing to provide unconditional support to the war effort. A letter addressed to the then Additional Secretary to the Government of Bengal, signed by Abdul Halim, Dharani Goswami, Gopen Chakravarty, Promode Dasgupta, Gopal Acharya, Ranendranath Basu, Abdul Momin, Niranjan Sen, Mohd Ismail and others from 249D, Bow Bazar Street, Calcutta, reads: "We urge upon the Government to realise that it is a race against time. The enemy is at our doors, and the Government should be well-aware that particularly in this province, there is a wide-spread fifth-columnist activity, busy sowing Pro-Japan or defeatist feeling among the masses. Unless the Government immediately gives full facilities to popular organisations like ours to pull their entire weight on the side of the cause of the United Nations and unless we could immediately mobilise all our leaders and cadres and distribute among the people in ceaseless agitation and organisation to counteract fifth-column propagation and to enthuse the people in defending their Motherland against Jap aggression, etc." (IB File No. 3D 99/42, Home (Pol) Cont:/1942 Bengal Government)

Once the bigger ones complied, the smaller fish followed suit. Communist workers from the districts, who were scattered in various prisons and detention camps all over Bengal, urged the Government to release them so they could actively form anti-Jap people's struggle. Here are a string of statements:

Statement of Babu Ballavi Bakshi:

"... I hold Communist views. My views regarding the present war is that every effort should be made by the Communist workers to oppose the Jap aggression which is knocking at our doors. In order to win the War, it is desirable that free scope should be given to the Communist and the anti-Fascist workers with the view to carrying on anti-Fascist propaganda. I am prepared to help the British Government in their war efforts, since it is admitted by Communist that this war is no longer an Imperialist War" (IB File No. 1240/42, Treatment of Communist who have been convicted of offences involving anti-war activity, but who may now announce a change in their attitude, and wish to assist the war-effort, Recorded by P Das Gupta, SI, DIB, Chinsurah, dated 27 June 1942, Hooghly Jail, p.71).

Statement of Anath Nath Ghosh:

"... I do not think that any Kishan movement should be launched at the present moment to embarrass the Government because such a movement will indirectly help the Jap or the German Government who are now against the British." (*Ibid*, Recorded by S Chatterjee, SI, DIB, Chinsurah, dated 24 June 1942, Hooghly Jail, p.69)

Statement of Chittaranjan Datta:

> ". . . I do not think that any labour movement should be launched so as to embarrass the war efforts of the British Government at the present moment. Labourers and Kishans of the country should now be united against the Fascist power." (*Ibid*, dated 2 July 1942, Hooghly Jail, p.74)

As a result of this change in attitude, the alien Government decided to release the Communists. S Dutta of the CID commented, "Communists are not necessarily terrorists, and the consideration on which it was decided not to order further release of terrorist prisoners need not necessarily apply to Communist prisoners" (*Ibid*, Continuous Note Sheet, CID, IB dated 27 April 1942, p.1).

The Government quite obviously felt elated. The ban on CPI was lifted on 23 July 1942. "As the CPI has promised to co-operate in the war effort, the Government decided to set them free," informed the Government Press Note. Finally, in the last month of 1942, P C Joshi met Sir Reginald Maxwell. Sir Reginald made certain observations about this young General Secretary and his action plan. "Joshi is concentrating on the appeal to patriotism. He wishes people to believe that they are fighting for freedom. He points out that only India can suffer from such things and finds this line of appeal effective in conversation with young men whom he gets to listen to him. The demand for National Government voiced by the 'People's War' is intended to appeal to this statement. So also the 'Unity Campaign' is based on it . . . Joshi was evidently confident that if National Government became a fact the Communist would dominate it with the aid of non-Gandhi elements, among which he includes Nehru, and in fact he expected Gandhi to take a back seat" (Government of India, Home Department File No. FN 7/15/42- Poll (I) 1942; extract from the report of the interview between P C Joshi and R M Maxwell, on 2 December 1942. This report was signed by Maxwell on 3 December 1942. Also see: Chaudhuri, Ashim Kumar, *Socialist Movement in India*, p.159).

Joshi, through his writings, had already started laying down the action-plan his Party would take in order to combat the enemy: "We shall send our members, sympathisers and supporters into the different branches of the fighting forces and specially train them so that they may inspire even the mercenaries recruited by the imperialist Government with the People's War spirit. We shall champion the cause of the soldiers, we shall expose their grievances, racial discrimination, high-handed treatment by their officers, lack of cultural rights and win public support for soldiers' demands and thus endeavour to create the atmosphere for real National army." (Government of India, Home Department File No. FN 7-5-42-Poll (I) 1942, Forward to Freedom: P C Joshi)

The Government seized upon the Communist's offer to take up arms and organised a programme for training a guerrilla army, to be composed largely of Communist volunteers. About 300 volunteers had congregated in a camp outside Poona to be instructed in guerrilla warfare under the supervision of Chinese and American Officers (Overstreet, p.206). However, this camp was abandoned mid-way.

Meanwhile, in 1942, negotiations with the Congress failed. The Cripps Mission went back to London empty handed, having been discarded by the Congress. The Nationalist forces had no option but to go for an all-out attack on the Government that had dragged India into the war without her consent. Thanks to the presence of the Allies, the Axis forces could now attack India. This necessitated the Congress meet in Bombay in August 1942, with Gandhi giving the call for 'Do or Die', and an ultimatum to the British to 'Quit India'.

Gandhi reiterated: "Everyone of you should from this moment onwards consider yourself a free man and woman and act as if you are free and are no longer under the heel of this Imperialism . . . I am not going to be satisfied with anything short of complete freedom . . . We shall do or die. We shall either free India or die in the attempt." (AICC Session, 8 August 1942, *Amrita Bazar Patrika*, 9 August 1942) The Government was quick to respond. The very next day, 9 August, all the principal leaders were arrested and the Congress

Party was banned under the Indian Criminal Law Amendment Act, 1908.

What followed was an unprecedented upsurge, with the masses taking the leadership into their own hands. The intensity of the movement in the initial stages reminded the rulers of the days of the Mutiny. People, together with the leaders who had gone underground, started forming liberated zones. Millions, thereafter, were poised to demand Independence, as they had never done before, as a non-negotiable goal, and every act of defiance and rebellion just fuelled the nationalist sentiment.

The Communists, on the contrary, were obliged to explain their opposition to National aspirations. To them, it was a People's War, and Britain being Russia's ally, they were in duty bound to stand by the Government in its war-effort. The Communist members who had joined the AICC meeting, Dr Ashraf, Sajjad Zaheer, Bal Krishna Sharma, had tried their best to dissuade the leadership from taking any radical steps but had failed (Chopra, P N, *Quit India Movement*, p.265). The Government, on its part, assured that "if any Communist members of the AICC are still in custody, and would be likely to oppose Congress Working Committee Resolution, if enabled to attend the meeting, it is suggested that the Provincial Governments should consider desirability of early release" (Government of India, Home Department File No. FN 7-15-42-Poll (I) 1942, Secret Letter No.7-2-42 Political (I) dated Delhi, 31 July 1942, from R Tottenham, Additional Secretary to the Government of India, see: Chaudhuri, p.148). But this did not work.

Having failed, Joshi and others started attacking the Congress resolution as retrograde. "After 9 days of labour, the CWC has brought forth an abortion. The resolution it has produced has bankruptcy writ large upon it. From the rut of inactivity it now seeks to lead the nation into the blind desperation and disaster." (*People's War*, 19 July 1942) N K Krishnan, in a pamphlet, National Unity for the defence of the Motherland, wrote, "The struggle for National unity and the unity campaign is not only the anti-thesis of the Congress struggle for sabotage and deadlock but its anti-dote. The Congress struggle campaign means disunity incarnate now and growing disunity as struggle develops . . . Our unity campaign cannot grow side by side with this disunity campaign but at its expense" (p.7).

As the Nationalistic wave surged, following the Congress resolution, some other groups, too, worked towards the same end – Independence. Previously, the Communists called these groups fifth-columnists. The most outstanding among them was Subhas Chandra Bose, who had escaped from the country, joined the Axis Powers, and was planning to enter India through the North-eastern corridor. Lambasting Subhas Chandra, or, as he was popularly called Netaji, became the favourite pastime of the Communists. Netaji was the lap-dog of Japanese Imperialism. "The Assam office of 'Jap-German Independence Association' published a message from Subhas Bose which glorifies acts of anarchy and sabotage as 'War of Independence'. The guerrillas are working destruction to Government property and railways. I now appeal to my countrymen to join the war of Independence with heart and soul. I specifically appeal to the Communist Party to rise to the occasion. We shall help in all respects" declares Subhas Bose, the so-called 'henchman' of Japanese Imperialism. The appeal will certainly not fall on deaf ears. The Communist Party will rise to the occasion and give the only reply which traitors and quislings have got from honest patriots. Bose's mercenary army of 'liberation', of rapine and plunder will feel the wrath and indignation of our people if it dare set foot on Indian soil to enact acts of pillage and robbery" (*People's War* on Subhas Bose, 10 January 1942).

Why did the Communists go against mainstream politics? If the Party records are to be believed, with Government patronage, sales of 'People's War' shot up by 124 per cent; it came in five languages in addition to six regional language newspapers. The total circulation reached 65,000 copies.

If the growth of the Party and its ancillary units in Andhra are taken as a sample, the figures below make an interesting read:

ORGANISATION	1942 (Members)	1945
Party members	796	7,000
Functionaries	300	700
Trade Union	10,000	40,000
Kishan Sabha	60,000	1,70,000
AGRICULTURAL		
Labour Union	10,000	30,000
Youth Organ	10,000	20,000
Mahila Sangha	3,000	15,000
Student Federation	6,000	9,000

PUBLISHING HOUSE

People's Publishing House, Bombay	–	English, Hindi, Urdu, Gujrati, Marathi publications
Prajashakti Publishing	–	Bezwada for Telegu Publishing
Deshabhmani Publishing	–	Calicut for Malayalam publication
Janashakti Publication	–	George Town, Madras for Tamil
Jangey Azadi Publishing	–	114 Mcleod Road, Lahore for Punjabi
National Book Agency	–	12 Bankim Chatterjee Street, Calcutta for Bengali

Another point that needs to be stressed is that all the auxiliary units, apparently non-political in its appeal, like, MARS, IPTA *et al*, were created to propagate the Party policy. In a Political Circular No. 105/43, dated 29 June 1943, one Comrade Annada Shankar Bhattacharya noted, "Bal Sangh should be the pioneer's organisation; an auxiliary mass organisation of the Party. We will make it as broad-based as possible but on a real political basis. Its programme must be anti-Japanese, National Defence and National unity on the basis of self-determination (Pakistan)" (IB File No. 282/39, Letters and circulars from the Secretary, Bengal Communist Party, SL 498, Part IX, Item 1685). Bal Sangh or Kishore Bahini was primarily a juvenile outfit, to work in conjunction with the Students' Federation with most of its members under fifteen years of age.

For some more figures 'The Way Out of the Crisis – Report on the decision taken by the Plenary Session of the Central Committee of the CPI, 10-24 February 1943 can be considered.

We have more than doubled our membership. We lost 29 old members but gained 4,448 new ones.

Party membership	–	9,219+ 8,816 auxiliaries in training for full membership (of these about 2,000 are whole-timers)
Party Publication	–	Central Headquarters, 26 pamphlets with 42,500 copies and 92.5 per cent were sold out.

Party fund Rs 5 lakhs

24,610	volunteers in Red Guards
1,97,629	workers in 240 Trade Unions
2,81,109	workers in Kishan Sabhas
25,822	women in Mahila Atmaraksha Samitis
6,400	kids in Bala Sanghams

Party Finances (Passed by the Central Committee of the CPI, at Bombay, 23 February 1943)

Cash-in-hand at the time of the legalisation of the Party	Rs 13,000+stocks of books, machinery, newsprint worth Rs 5,500
– Issued a call for	Rs 30,000 for People's War
– realised	Rs 31,000
From August 1942–January 1943	Rs 6,500 in regional donation + Rs 29,000 as special donation

– Call for Rs 2 Lakh Fund by Central Committee Plenum, September 1942

Actual Cash realised Rs 3,50,900 + pending promises of Rs 1,50,000

Three provinces reached the figure of a lakh and more – Andhra, Kerala and Bengal.

Centre's Share	– Rs 1,80,000
Total Realisation	– Rs 2,65,000
Party's Expenses	– Rs 21,000
Machinery and Equipment	– Rs 30,000
Paper Stock	– Rs 2 lakhs
Cash Balance	– Rs 15, 000 ('Lid Off', (Chari, A S K, *Andhra Anti-Communism*)

The Party had individual donors, e.g. Snehangshu Acharya, who, having inherited his father's property in 1944, rendered substantial financial help to the Party. He donated one lakh rupees to the Party fund besides Rs 200/- monthly for the rent of the Provincial Committee, 121 Lower Circular Road, Calcutta (IB File No. 886/42, (History Sheet Folder), SL No. 125, Snehangshu Acharya).

In fact, the General Secretary had good reasons to be elated, for the CPI was clearly thriving under him, during the war years, while everything else slumped. This was also the time when those who had anything to do with the Nationalist Parties were being hounded, but the Communists lived peaceably.

Joshi guided not just the People's War Policy, but also the Nationality Theory in support of the concept of Pakistan.

CHAPTER THREE

The Theory of Nationality

The All India Muslim League, right from its very inception in 1906, was a Party of big Zaminders, Nawabs, Knights and Pirzadas. The Party projecting itself as the vanguard of the Muslims in India had hardly any connection with the down-trodden masses. Yet, it went on receiving undue importance from the Government. It was a ploy of the Government to use the League as a pawn against the Nationalist forces. They had already started pursuing a 'divide and rule policy'. They met, for example, the Muslims' demand for a separate electorate. Yet, the commoners hardly took the All India Muslim League seriously.

Mohammed Ali Jinnah, the former ambassador of Hindu-Muslim Unity, returned to India in the mid-thirties and took over the reins of this elite grouping known as the Muslim League. Once a Congressman, Jinnah abhorred Gandhi's politics of mass agitation, being a constitutionalist by nature. Gandhi's ascend in the Congress meant the end of Jinnah's political career, at least within the Congress. Thus he had moved to England, and had become a non-entity in terms of Indian politics. It was only after persuasion from the Muslim leaders to take control of the League that he accepted to return to Indian politics; he came back to organise and consolidate the League so that during the transfer of power, his community shall not miss out.

The League's claim of being the representative of the Muslim toilers in India was soon put to test in the Election of 1937. Contesting the separate Muslim seats, the League was able to secure only 4.8 per cent of the total Muslim votes. It was thus unable to form a Government in any of the Muslim majority provinces. In Punjab, it contested in 7 and won 2 out of the total 84 Muslim seats. In Sind, the figure was 3 out of 33 and in Bengal, 38 out of 117. The Congress, on the other hand, contested in 1,161 seats in the General Constituencies and won 716. It had a clear majority in six out of eleven provinces in British India and emerged as the single largest Party in three provinces, in the process routing the Hindu Mahasabha in Punjab. It had, however, a poor show as regards Muslim seats. Having contested in 56 out of 482 Muslim seats, the Congress won only 28, but was unable to secure a single Muslim seat in the UP, Bengal and Punjab. It only fared well in the NWFP, where it was due to the 'Frontier Gandhi' factor. The chunk of the Muslim seats went to the rainbow-coalition led by the Unionists in Punjab and to the Krishak Praja Party in Bengal.

Having failed dismally to establish their sway over the masses in the Election, the Muslim League resorted to Communalism. Criticising the Congress ministries formed in various provinces of tormenting the Muslims, the League played the communal card. The status of minority would not solve Muslim problems. In fact, Muslims were not minorities; they were a nation by themselves, distinct from the Hindus in all walks of life. Thus the Muslims in India needed a homeland where they could lead a life on the basis of Islamic teachings. India was not one nation, but two. Akhand Hindustan was a ploy of the bania Hindus to perpetually keep the Muslims under their heels and continue exploiting them.

The demand for a separate nation, which later came to be called Pakistan, found utterance on the Lahore Declaration of the Muslim League, 23 March, 1940.

". . . geographically contiguous units . . . demarcated into the regions which should be constituted, with such territorial re-adjustments as may be necessary, that the areas in which the Muslims are numerically in a majority, as in the North-Western and Eastern Zones of India, should be grouped to constitute Independent States in which the constituent units shall be autonomous and sovereign." This was to remain the League's agenda for the next seven years.

The League curiously found an ally in the Communist Party. The Communist Party after being legalised in 1942 had gained strength in the absence of the Congress and other Nationalist forces. This was apart from preaching the People's War line, brought forward its nationality theory based upon Soviet model. It was the brain-child of Dr Gangadhar Adhikari, the major theoretician within the Party, who discussed it in his 'Pakistan and National Unity'. The treatise held the League, ". . . is no longer feudal-reactionary, no longer just a willing tool of Imperialism. It is now an industrial bourgeois leadership, which is no more just an adjunct of Imperialism. In fact, the Muslim League is to the Muslim peoples what the Indian National Congress is to the Indian masses in general". As we know, this opinion was very close to Jinnah's question of 'parity' at the Shimla Conference of 1945. Be that as it may, in 1942 the League enjoyed only 4.8 per cent support of the Muslim masses in terms of votes polled in the last election.

Adhikari continued, "Wherever people of Muslim faith living together in a territorial unit form a nationality . . . they certainly have the right to autonomous state existence". Actually, the demand for Pakistan, to the Communists, agreed with the demand of other nationalities for the right to self-determination.

"Since 1940, our Party began to see that the so-called communal problem – especially Hindu-Muslim problem in India was really a problem of growing nationalities and that it could only be solved on the basis of the recognition of the right of self-determination to the point of political secession, of the Muslim Nationalities, and in fact of all nationalities." This Nationality theory held that India was a family of Nations, all of them having the right to secede. Joshi explained the Party's position more clearly, "In order to say that all Indians must stand together against British rule, *it is not at all necessary to say that India is one nation* (italics ours). Sticking to such a concept only multiplies problems instead of helping to solve; it blinds one to reality and rouses fears of

Hindu domination" (Adhikari, Gangadhar, *Pakistan & National Unity*). Joshi and others identified 17 such units within India who were nations and thus had the right to secede, forming independent states outside the Indian Union.

This new line of the Party was totally different from what it had preached till then. An All India Kishan Conference was held in the local Town Hall at Comilla on 18 May 1938. Shamsul Huda of the CPI had urged the Muslims to reflect on whether the fight was a religious or a political one. He had said that the Congress was the organisation to gain Independence for India. The Muslim League, on the other hand, was a party of big Zaminders, Khan Bahadurs, and Nawab Bahadurs and did not have peasants and the poor among its members. They were not fighting for the interest of the Muslims but had their own interest in mind (IB File No. 378/28; Shamsul Huda, p.60). But its policy changed during its People's War period.

Joshi went further, "We Communists say, let us get back to the India as it was before the British conquered us and on lines along which we were ourselves growing. Our concept of 17 free homelands inhabited by the peoples of Baluchistan, Pathanland, Sind, Western Punjab, Central Punjab, Hindustan, Rajasthan, Gujerat, Maharashtra, Karnataka, Andhra, Kerala, Tamil Nad, Orissa, Bengal, Assam and Bihar within a free India is the most natural one for the free development of our peoples and the only way to solve our difficulties and liquidate our differences. Rather than dividing up India, it creates the basis for building a happy India. It is criminal to seek to preserve the unity of British made India as it would be split up the unity of India" (Joshi, *For The Final Bid For Power: Freedom Programme of Indian Communist*, p.9). And again, ". . . Just when our people were becoming modern nations, the British conquered us and disrupted our national development . . . The concept of homelands comes most naturally to us Indians . . . It is no accident that we call our homelands Desh, or Rashtra or Mulk in our languages. It is no accident that the great Bankim sang of Sapth Koti (seven-crore Bengalis), when Joshi sang of freedom. It is no accident that when the poet Tagore sang Jana

Gana Mana, he sang about 'Punjab, Sind, Gujerat, Maratha, Dravida, Utkala, Banga' Nations. These 17 peoples are much more than cultural units. They are growing nations. They consist of our peoples as they were till the British came and conquered disrupted them" (*Ibid*, p.289).

This Nationality Theory was based on the pre-supposition that 1) the states demarcated really wanted to secede and no longer believed in being part of the Indian life, and, 2) once given the right to secede, they would join together to form a sort of United States of India on Soviet lines. But as we are aware, in Russia, although the right of self-determination was granted to the many nationalities on paper, in practice it was the Red Army which was instrumental in keeping all the regions together. The Indian position was completely different. Here there were numerous political groups with different agenda. Propagation of such ideas of separation would invite them to flirt with such ideas.

Apart from the Muslim League with its demand for Pakistan, there was the Scheduled Castes' Federation with a demand for Acchutsthan, Justice Party in the South, with a demand for Dravidastan, certain formation within the Aboriginals with a vague Adivasisthan, the Sikhistan, later to be propagated by the Akali Party and so forth. None cared about getting into anti-British struggle, but all were ready for their pound of flesh once the Imperial masters decided to transfer power. The result would have been a perpetual civil war and utter balkanisation of India. Moreover, seeking an India of the pre-British era was to look backward, for it was contrary to the idea not only of a modern nation-state, but also of unity keeping the diverse nature of the state. This is what the educated segment of society, with men like Tagore, Tilak and Gandhi, had so long nurtured.

What about the 500-odd Princely states? Must the right of self-determination be extended to them?

The Communist persisted with their new-found solution of the Indian question. Sajjad Zaheer, the Oxford-bred Communist put a question to the Congress, "How can they (Congress) deny the rights of the Muslims living in compact areas and in big majorities to frame their own future, to be the masters of their own destiny? Is it conceivable that the Frontier Pathans, or Baluchis or Sindhi or Punjabi Muslims can be kept together in a free India against their wish? Let Congressmen give a clear answer" (Zaheer, Sajjad, *A Case for Congress-League Unity*, p.11). That a Sindhi or a Punjabi or a Bengali Muslim had much more cultural commonalities with a Sindhi or a Punjabi or a Bengali Hindu than with his co-religionist from a different part of the country, apart from sharing the same religion was totally overlooked, perhaps consciously.

There were other contradictions within the theory itself. For example, Bengal was identified as a Nation; East Bengal formed a special problem. Here, generally speaking, the Muslim population was more than 60 per cent. Within the framework of a common nationality, the Muslim peasantry of Eastern Bengal has a distinct cultural complex of its own which has left an impression on Eastern Bengal as a separate entity. Meaning Bengal is a nation but East Bengal is a different entity as it has Majority as Muslims. Thus the common grounds of culture, language, etc become secondary! It must be said that the Communist were making matters much worse!

The Communists shall remain confident about their theory till the very end, i.e. August 1947. The support to Pakistan would also be followed diligently. P C Joshi would himself declare with satisfaction that, "We are the only non-Muslim organisation that has voluntarily accepted and popularised the demand of the Muslim peoples to be sovereign in their own majority homelands. We have done this despite the suspicions of the League leadership about our Party and despite slanders against us in the League press. Every serious Leaguer knows it and respects us for this in a manner that he respects no other non-Muslim. No Muslim can look us in the face and say that we have not suffered and fought for his cause more than he himself, done in that section of our freedom struggle to which he himself had no access because of the way our people stands divided among themselves today" (Joshi, *For the Final Bid for Power*, p.96). This support would not just be restricted to verbal encouragements; it would be actively followed in practice.

The League, being a bit sceptical, had reasons to feel happy.

CHAPTER FOUR

Propaganda for Pakistan

We have already suggested that the Communists did not limit themselves to theoretical support to the idea of Pakistan. It actually buttressed the demand, especially among the non-Muslim masses, besides others. In the period between 1943 and 45, the Communists participated, in strength, in various functions and meetings organised by the Muslim League to proclaim their demand for Pakistan.

The line to be followed had already been decided in the Enlarged Plenum of the Central Committee of the CPI held at Bombay, during its September Session, 1942. In response to the slogan for Congress-League unity, it was agreed to set up a Provisional Government for the successful defence of the country and freedom. The position already taken by the Congress as well as by the Muslim League as regards the question of the rights of Muslims to self-determination in certain areas, with good will on both sides, could afford a basis for immediate settlement.

It was noted, "On the basis of these two slogans, the campaign for Unity must be run among the Muslims as well as Hindu masses. To the Hindu masses we must explain that what is just in this Pakistani demand, namely, the right of Muslim nationalities to autonomous state existence, including the right of separation must be conceded. It will give us unity now and lead to freedom . . . Similarly we must get the Congress-minded people to recognise the urgency of the Congress conceding the right of self-determination of the Muslim nationalities and thus hasten the achievement of Congress-League Unity. To the Muslim masses, we must show that Muslim Independence can only come by joining with the Hindus and Congress for joint action" (Krishnan, (Ed.), *National Unity for the Defence of the Motherland*, p.21).

Even the Party organ also suggested to concentrate on, "showing – the basically progressive character of League and Mr Jinnah. That it is a far cry from the loyalist League and today it must be driven into the heads of the People's War patriots. This is all the more necessary in the light of the Nationalist press using every move of the Muslim League in Punjab and elsewhere to prove that League and specially Mr Jinnah are reactionary and tools of British Imperialism" (IB File No. 849/42(i); No. 4155/B-1261 (spare copies) People's War, intercepted letter written by Arvinda Dutta (spare copies), recipient unknown).

It would be wrong to think that the Party started the League's demand for Pakistan only after it had adopted its People's War Policy. Some examples will pass muster.

Take the meeting held at Shraddhananda Park (Calcutta), for example, on 27 May 1941. Ostensibly, it aimed at "Hindu-Muslim Students' Peace". Nikhil Maitra of the Federation presided over the proceedings, while the speakers were Samin Hore, Nazir Ahmed of the 'Weekly Medina', A S Khan, late Assistant Secretary of the Bengal Provincial Muslim Students' League, Sadequr Rahman, Secretary, Bengal Students' Federation Muslim League, Jafar Ali Mazumdar, Secretary, North Calcutta Students' Federation (CPI), and others.

Maitra in his presidential address said, "We should not condemn our Muslim friends for their proposal for Pakistan. If we consider calmly and soberly we shall understand that every nation has got its own right to culture his own religion, education etc. So if we agree to the proposal for creating Pakistan, we would also get similar privileges from our Moslem brethren". Sadequr Rahman said that if the Hindu brethren accept their (i.e. the League's) proposal for Pakistan, the Muslim too shall give all sorts of privileges to the Hindus in return. Jafar Ali Mazumdar reminded that if the Congress or the Hindu Mahsabha do not stand against the Muslim League, there would be no communal tension (IB File No. 3637/37 Pt. II, Bengal Provincial Students' Federation, p.203-203A).

Once the Party had taken an official stand to support Pakistan, the Communists started working jointly with the League. Some instances will bear that out:

Pakistan Day Celebrations, Lohajung, March 1944: observed at Lohajung, Baraikhali, Rekhabi Bazar, (East Bengal) a procession set out and a public meeting was held under the presidentship of Nur Hussain. Suranjan Bannerjee, a Communist worker, spoke in support of the demand for Pakistan and made an appeal to the League leaders to press for the release of Congress leaders. The meeting terminated with shouts of 'Pakistan Zindabad' (Pakistan Day celebrations, *Morning News*, 29 March 1944). Letter to the Editor, *People's War*, 25 March 1944, from Phani Guha, the Dacca District Committee of the CPI, 15, Court House Street, Dacca: "That the demand for Pakistan and India's freedom movement are not contradictory but have roots in the same freedom urge of the people of India, was expressed when Pakistan Day was observed in Dacca City on 23 March. The day before, our comrades approached the Muslim League leaders, both veteran and young, for joint work, so that the day would be observed as one of unity. A squad approached the Muslim students and requested them to explain to the masses the real significance of the day. Our comrades were invited to speak in the next day's open-air meeting. In the afternoon about 500 people gathered at Pakistan Park . . . Comrade Samin Hore of the CPI spoke on the necessity of Congress-League Unity" (IB File No. 849/42(i), People's War, p.98).

Pakistan Day was observed in Chittagong under the auspices of District Muslim Students' League. Houses, hostels and shops were decorated with League flags which were distributed by the Muslim students. A mammoth crowd of 10,000 men attended a meeting in the Muslim Hall. Siddique Ahmed Chudhury, Md Yusuf, Comrade Jashoda Chakravarty, Secretary, Communist Party, Chittagong, Lufte Ahmed Chowdhury, Abdul Majid and Kazi Najmul Huq were the key speakers.

Comrade Kalpana Dutt (This was the same Kalpana Dutt of Chittagong Armory Raid fame whom P C Joshi married in 1943), President, Nari Samiti and Comrade Madhu Singh, Secretary, All India Students' Federation, congratulated the organisation and supporters of Pakistan Scheme. The meeting ended with cries of 'Pakistan Zindabad' and 'Muslim League Zindabad' (Pak Day at Different Centres: Chittagong, *Star of India*, 25 March 1944).

In a letter written to Annada Shankar Bhattacharya, Secretary, Bengal Provincial Students' Federation, Madhu Singh described the kind of support the local League was providing to the meetings of the Communists. "League – actively co-operating with us, is always pressing to call joint meetings. Two meetings were held in town. One, on the behalf of Students' Federation and another jointly. Attendance was 400 and 300 respectively. President of both the meetings were League leaders. In the latter meeting 'Unity Flag' was hoisted by League Secretary, amidst unity slogans." Singh also added that they had planned 12 such meetings in the district, and 1,000 leaflets had already been distributed (IB File No. 810/36(i), SL No. 129, Hirendranath Mukherjee, Extract Folder Pt. I, Date of interception: 10 August 1944, Chittagong, date of the letter unknown, p.280).

A joint relief board of students representing Barishal District Muslim League and Barishal District Students' Federation was formed, with Mozammel Huq and Sushil Sen as Joint Secretaries. Their role was to co-ordinate the activities of different medical units working in the district and render help to distressed students (Students' Relief Board, *Star of India*, 24 May 1944).

Here are some examples of the Communist' passionate eagerness for the success of Gandhi-Jinnah talks, where success is to be measured on League's terms:

A unity rally was held in the Park Circus Maidan, Calcutta, presided over by Khan Bahadur Abdul Hameed Choudhury, MLA. Comrade Bhawani Sen, the General Secretary of the Bengal Provincial Communist Party moved a resolution saying that as the political deadlock prevailing in India was most detrimental to the country, Hindus and Muslims should unite and support Rajaji's formula (i.e. acceptance of Pakistan demand). Other speakers included Muazzamuddin Hussain Chowdhury, MLC, Sadhan Gupta, President of the Bengal Students' Federation and Shamsul Huda, Vice-President of the Aligarh Muslim University Union (Unity Rally Meeting, *Star of India*, 4 August 1944).

A resolution expressing the ardent desire of Orissa Kishans for successful conclusion of the Gandhi-Jinnah talks was passed at the Pakistan rally held in Cuttack, with Comrade Biswanath Mukherjee as president. It eventually failed. The resolution requested Gandhiji to accept self-determination for Muslim nationalities as their birth-right and an appeal was made to Jinnah to join hands with the Congress for the release of Congress leaders and establishment of a National Government (Pakistan Rally in Cuttack, *Star of India*, 6 September 1944).

The Secretary of the CPI, Andhra Unit sent the following telegram to Gandhiji and Jinnah: "Under the auspices of the Andhra Communist Party meetings and demonstrations held throughout the province form 1st to the 17th (September 1944) supporting principle of self-determination . . . two lakh people from 750 villages and towns of the province express their keen desire for success Gandhi-Jinnah talks (Communist Wire to Mr Gandhi and Mr Jinnah, *Star of India*, 18 August 1944).

In March 1943, All India Students' Federation held a meeting at the Calcutta University Institute. The agenda of the meeting was as under:

  i) Release of Gandhiji
  ii) Formation of an All Party National Government

Khwaja Nazimuddin of the Muslim League sent a message stating, "If the Bengal Provincial Students' Federation succeeded in creating public opinion in favour of adopting the principle of self-determination that would not only lead to unity between the two communities but bring about the release of Mr Gandhi and other leaders" (Calcutta Students' Demands, *Amrita Bazar Patrika*, 3 March 1943).

Similarly a convention of the Surma Valley Students' Federation was held from 25 to 27 November 1944 to discuss the viewpoints of Gandhi and Jinnah on the issue of national sovereignty and recognition of Muslim rights of self-determination and Congress-League Unity. An appeal was sent by Debnath Dutta, Surma Valley Students' Federation, Sylhet, dated 18 November 1944 to Anwar Hossain, Secretary, Bengal Provincial Muslim Students' League, to offer inspiring and educative message which would help the participants march forward with the banner of freedom, peace and progress.

Similar appeals were sent to (IB File No. 810/36(i), SL No.129, Hirendranath Mukherjee, Extract Folder, Pt. I, p.285):

Abul Hashim, Secretary, Bengal Provincial Muslim League

Gopal Haldar, Editor, 'Parichaya' (A Communist Monthly)

Prof Hiren Mukherjee

S Mazumdar, Editor, 'Arani'

The Jinnah Day was observed in Dacca with all ceremony on 31 December 1945. In the evening, a public meeting was held at the Pakistan Park, with Dr Abani Bhusan Rudra, Professor of Dacca University, as president. Ali Ahsan, Jnan Chakravarty, Secretary, Dacca Communist Party, Abdul Jabbar and Shamsul Huq spoke on the life of Jinnah. Dr Rudra, in his presidential speech referred to the sacrifice, anti-imperialist feelings and firm faith in the ideology of Jinnah. He also appealed to the youth of India to follow the ideals of Jinnah (Jinnah Day Observed at Dacca, *Star of India*, 2 January 1945).

An Islamic Library was opened in the Muslim League Office, Dacca by Mahmud Hossain, Provost, Fazlul Huq Muslim Hall on Jinnah Day. During his opening speech, Mahmud Hossain hoped the library would really meet the needs of the Bengali Muslims. Ranesh Dasgupta, Secretary, Dacca District Progressive Writers' Association stressed the need for introducing Islamic culture and civilisation in India (Islamic Library, *Star of India*, 2 January 1945).

To celebrate Jinnah's birthday, a public meeting was called in the Islamia College Hall, Lahore, with Mian Bashir Ahmed, MLA, as president. Ashiq Batalavi, while addressing the meeting recalled Dr Iqbal's remarks, "Mr Jinnah is the only Mussalman in India who is not purchasable and is incorruptible". He further said that within a short span of few years, Jinnah had brought a revolution in Muslim India. Balraj Mehta, a prominent member of Punjab's Students' Federation said, "Mr Jinnah is anti-imperialist and not anti-Congress. His life has been a relentless struggle for achievement of three objectives – Freedom of India, Hindu-Muslim understanding and the birth right of the Muslims, i.e. Pakistan (Mr Jinnah's Birthday, *Star of India*, 5 January 1945).

The first meeting of the Pakistan Politics Club was held on 30 March 1945 at the Islamia College Hall, Calcutta with Lt Col Sir Hasan Suhrawardy in the chair. Abul Hashim, Habibullah Bahar and Prof Hiren Mukherjee spoke on 'Pakistan – A struggle for Independence' (Pakistan Politics Club, *Star of India*, 29 May 1945). This was not the first occasion, when the leading theoretician of the Bengal Committee, Hiren Mukherjee, spoke on this subject.

A series of lectures on current and international affairs from 14 -18 March 1944 was convened by the Bengal unit of the Students' Federation with Annada Shankar Bhattacharya, Ranajit Guha, Gita Mukherjee, Tarun Bose, Ashoke Roy as its main organisers. It was held in the Indian Association Hall, Calcutta. On 14 March, Prof Hiren Mukherjee spoke on the subject, "Pakistan and Indian Unity" (IB File No. 810/36(i), S L No. 129, Hirendranath Mukherjee, Extract Folder Pt. I, p.265).

A meeting with approximately 2,500 people attending of which more than 600 were students, under the auspices of All India Students' Federation (AISF) was held in Calcutta. Santosh Dasgupta, Umapada Ganguly and Sidhukar Das, the President, appealed to the students to unite and save education; they urged the people to release the leaders and thereby unite the Nation to achieve National Government. Afluddin Ahmed, Joint Secretary, Bengal Provincial Muslim Students' League also addressed the meeting and said that the Congress-League unity alone on the basis of Pakistan could lead to free India (Students' Meeting at Calcutta, *Amrita Bazar Patrika*, 27 March 1945).

The AISF organised a debate on the Pakistan issue at Mohammad Ali Park Conference Pandal, Calcutta with a number of students from different universities of India participating. Nausher Ali, Speaker of the Bengal Legislative Assembly, chaired the meet (Debate on Pakistan Issue, *Amrita Bazar Patrika*, 1 January 1945).

"If we fail to unite and take the future of the country in our own hands, Imperialism will force on us a Constitution on the basis of that Coupland Scheme, which will be worse than the Communal Award . . .," emphasised Dr Z A Ahmed (Communist) presiding over a students' meeting at Lahore in February 1945. Raja Ghajanfar Ali, a Muslim League MLA said, "we can neither get Pakistan nor Swaraj without Hindu-Muslim Unity. Pakistan presupposes India's freedom which can be won only if we present a united front against present rulers" (Congress-League Unity, Pakistan Pre-supposed Indian Freedom, *Amrita Bazar Patrika*, 7 February 1945).

800 delegates from various branches of the Communist Party, throughout Great Britain, representing 50,000 party members listened to a debate on the Labour Governments policy towards India at the Annual Congress held in London on 25 November 1945. A great ovation was given to S S Mirajkar, fraternal delegate from CPI. Mirajkar, in his speech said, "It is true that our main national organisations – Congress and the Muslim League – hold divergent views on the future of India, but while you admire the Congress as a premier organisation of the freedom movement, you should not dismiss the League as a minority, for its driving force is the Muslim masses who have awakened consciousness of their nationhood. The Communists of India support the demand of Muslims for their right of self-determination" (British Communist Demand India's Freedom/Full Support for Pak; Muslim Masses Behind League, *Morning News*, 27 November 1945).

Lucknow, February 1946: The Congress-League unity on the basis of the Right to self-determination of Indian nationalities for wresting freedom for the country was emphasised at a public meeting held in

the Ganga Prasad Memorial Hall under the auspices of the Lucknow
Communist Party. Dr Z A Ahmed presided. Shafiq Ahmed Naqvi
pointed out that the question whether India was to have a federal
constitution, a union of free and sovereign states or two centres should
only be decided if the Indian Nationalities were given the right to freely
choose their own course of action (Communist for a Common Front,
The Pioneer, 1 February 1946).

From the above, it can be deduced that the Communists used its
student wing, All India Students' Federation, most for creating a popular
campaign in support to the Pakistan demand amongst the youth and
the intelligentsia. It was Joshi's brain-child and accordingly a *secret
instruction* dated 15 December 1944 was sent to Provincial Communist
Parties, discussing the pros and cons of the students' movement and
providing a guideline for the same. The following excerpts should be
enough:

THE STUDENTS' FRACTION: P C JOSHI
On the failure of Gandhi-Jinnah talks

According to the Communist, the root of the trouble is in the
very concept of the so-called one nation theory. Actually the
Congress Socialist Party slogans – 'India is One Nation' – are at
its root. It smacked of Hindu chauvinism. The problem was the
Congress did not see League as a partner in freedom movement.
On the other hand, Pakistan was an Independent freedom
movement.

The 1920's belonged to Gandhi, so did 1930, but 1944 belongs
to us. Some national awakening of Muslims was found in Muslim
League. From rights to equal rights. Muslim intelligentsia with
League. By and by Khilafat and Congress Muslims join the
League.

India is one against the British but not on the basis of a Nation.
This means disrupting the freedom movement you have yourself
built. Two Nations and Hindu Domination.

Gandhi makes advance from his old position – No going back. Equality (with Muslims) accepted but not freedom (of Muslims). League must be showed that nothing to fear for freedom movement.

AGITATION
Make Congress accept Pakistan as freedom demand
Persuade the Leaguers to make democratic struggle

TASK
Make League and Congress boys understand each other's position

Get Congress and League boys against CSP and Hindu Mahasabha

Prevent Leaguers going anti-Hindu

SLOGANS
How can students help in National Unity?

Through mutual discussion, allay mutual suspicion and take to joint work – Bengal Relief.

HOW WE HAVE TO TALK WITH
CONGRESS STUDENTS
Gandhiji accepts separation if people want,

League most representative organisation of Muslims,

No withdrawal of Gandhi-Rajaji formula.

AN EXPLANATION
Pakistan is a demand for freedom of Muslim nationalities to rule in their own homelands. Explain this: a right which Congress has been demanding from the British Government. As Congress roused national consciousness in the country as a whole against the British Imperialism, similarly League roused the consciousness of the Muslims. They came late in the National Movement. League went through same stages of development as Congress (Liberal-

Dominion Status-Independence-Democratic Rights) League (Separate Electorates-Two Federations-Pakistan). Congress rightly claims to speak on behalf of Indian as it roused the Indian people, similarly League on behalf of the Muslims . . . Hindu Nationalities cling together as growing under one National Movement. Similarly Muslim Nationalities under League . . . We are giving them their Homelands and not our Homelands.

Jinnah's Position: Changing Pakistan; not Pan-Islamism. Pakistan would be a democratic state. Recognise it as a freedom demand. Then we can demand the freedom of Sikhs and Bengali Hindus. If the Congress-League unity is not today, what is in the future for us? Hindu Mahasabha leaders coming to the top with slogans of civil war – takes British support. It is a question of country divided into two camps, which Congress has been trying to eradicate. It makes Congress weak. No question of attacking Jinnah. If you do, it means playing into the hands of Mahasabha.

In August Resolution (Quit India), Jinnah does not object to Independence but of United India. Therefore, Jinnah asks what Independence to Muslim peoples? The fear of Hindu domination, Muslim interest would not be jeopardised.

HOW WE TALK TO MUSLIM LEAGUERS

". . . how can you get it without co-operation of Hindus and Congress, Congress your necessary ally.

Boundaries: In the name of freedom, you cannot grasp other's territories. It is necessary to have Sikhs (whole of Punjab) and United Bengal (whole of Bengal) but for that you have to convince them on the basis of justice.

SLOGANS

"Accept Self-determination-Gandhi ki Jai-Jinnah ki Jai" (IB File No. 848/36, Bengal Provincial Students' Federation, p.1196-2000).

Thus AISF started actively spreading the Nationality theory among students and continued to work jointly with the Muslim League's Students League and Federation. On its eighth Conference, 21 January 1945, the AISF welcomed friendly relations between the branches of the AISF and the All India Muslim Students' Federation, notably in Punjab and Bengal – established through joint work for Bengal Relief and for Congress-League Unity on the eve of the Gandhi-Jinnah talks. It hoped that this friendly relation will continue despite the failure of the Gandhi-Jinnah talks in the common interests of both. It appealed to the Muslim Students' Federation to take part in a friendly discussion in student ranks on the problem of Congress-League unity to evolve a common outlook and find a basis for the final settlement (IB File No. 848/36, Bengal Provincial Students' Federation, p.1213-14).

Along with this propaganda for Pakistan, Joshi continued with his 'Trojan-Horse' policy. The organisations that he badly needed under his control were AITUC and the Kishan Sabha to project his Party as the vanguard of the workers and peasants. The result was mixed.

The 20th Session of the All India Trade Union Congress met at Nagpur on 1 May 1943 with more than 400 delegates participating. The Communist section, led by Bankim Mukherjee and Somnath Lahiri moved a resolution declaring that the opposition of the British Government could be successfully overcome by active national unity based on Hindu-Muslim understanding. They urged upon all political parties and organisations to accept self-determination so that doubts and suspicions might be dispelled from the mind of the Muslim League brethren and the path opened for an irresistible demand for a National Government. They also urged upon political parties to devise a constitution based on the principles of self-determination and social justice. These two resolutions were strongly opposed by the other section of the Trade Union Congress, especially Mrinal Kanti Bose. He said that the Communist resolutions were not consistent with the principles and policies of the AITUC, which always stood for the unity of the workers and did not recognise the communities as unit for building a constitution or a series of constitutions. The Communist resolutions were rejected (All India Trade Union Congress, *Amrita Bazar Patrika*, 7 May 1943).

Success, however, came in case of the Kishan Sabha.

The All India Kishan Sabha was formed by Swami Sahajanand Saraswati, a peasant leader of Bihar in 1936. It was a peasants' organisation working on peasants issues. The Communist had joined the Sabha with help of the Congress Socialists. Now with the CSP gone underground due to the War, the Communists tried to take over the Sabha from within.

On 27 February 1945, Sahajanand being the President of the Sabha took disciplinary action against the entire central office of the Bombay Kishan Sabha, the whole of Bengal Sabha as, according to him, "they deliberately flouted the Sabha's orders and decision. The Sabha forbade by a specific resolution opening of the Pakistan question and doing propaganda in any form either for or against it. But they have gone on doing the same despite repeated warning and thus used the platforms and organs of the Sabha in favour of the CPI's policy" (Bengal Sabha Suspended by Kishan Sabha President, *Amrita Bazar Patrika*, 28 February 1945). But Sahajanand was fighting a lost battle. The opposition within the Sabha was stiff, for by that time the Communists had infiltrated heavily and had created such a situation that it was Sahajanand who had to tender his resignation from the Sabha.

The statement he issued was fairly long. "I am constrained to admit that during these long twenty months of mine has been the mere crying in the wilderness. The more I have laboured to better the condition, the worse have they (Communist) become and that domination has grown more pronounced. Every institution must be used to propagate its policies, they maintain, and the Kishan Sabha cannot escape that obvious fate. True, so far we have passed/agreed resolutions though after hard labour to withstand their extreme pressure to foist their Policy on the Sabha. But in actual practice they have strained their every nerve to give those resolutions full Communist colours. If possible, to tear and twist them, if necessary and ultimately to flout and defy them when there has remained no alternative left. The dictates of the party must be fulfilled, cost what it might. *Thus, the Kishan Sabha has been sought to be turned into a mere appendage of the Communist Party of India* (italics added). The Sabha has never called this war a People's War, but they have dragged our platform into that mire. We have never sought to arrogate only to ourselves true patriotism even in the name of the Sabha. The Sabha did ask three years back all its units and responsible individuals not to open the Pakistan question in any form, either for or against it, but they have deliberately used the organs of the Sabha to propagate the Pakistan policy of their party . . . Last December, at Calcutta, we appealed to the Congressmen to join the Sabha and I asked the Communist comrades to be ready for the implications of that appeal. Consistently with our position as the Kishans, I wanted to go to the furthest level to meet the honest patriots and Congressmen to ally their fears and misgivings and thus to pave the way for their freely joining the Kishan Sabha. But our comrades seem in no mood to accept this. Because in that they sense the danger to their present absolute majority in the Sabha. The spectre of weakening their hold over it is haunting in their mind." (Sahajanand Resigns Kishan Sabha Presidentship/ Communist Domination Over Body Too Much for Him, *Amrita Bazar Patrika*, 4 March 1945)

The communists followed their Trojan horse method in case of smaller Nationalities too. With the All India Gorkha League, they were successful up to a point. The Central Committee of the All India Gorkha League, which met on 13 May 1944 at Darjeeling, elected Comrade Ratan Lal Brahman as one of its Vice-Presidents and Comrade Ganesh Lal Subba (both of them were members of the CPI) as one its Assistant Secretaries. The inclusion of these two communists in the Gorkha League gave the impression that the Gorkhas, like the Muslim League, were sympathetic to the CPI. Some of the younger members of the Gorkha League, though they had little idea of what communism meant, were inclined to it all right. Dambar Singh Gurung, President of Gorkha

League, was at that point trying to bring all Gorkhas in his fold. The aim and objective of the Gorkha League was to establish political rights of the Gorkhas in India. Gurung even presided over a public meeting of the CPI in 1943 (IB File No. 558/46 Part II, Ratan Lal Brahman, Item 3(f); copy of report dated 17 November 1944 submitted by DIO (I) from District Intelligence Branch, Darjeeling). From the platform of the Gorkha League, the Communists demanded the creation of a separate homeland for the Gorkhas, to be called Gorkhalistan. The idea was to attract as much support as possible to their fold by strengthening their Party's presence. Ganesh Lal Subba sent a Memorandum to Gandhi and Jinnah, dated 12 August 1944, signed by, apart from him, Dambar Singh Gurung and Ratan Lal Brahman, to claim the right of self-determination for the Gorkhas.

"The Gorkhas living in such contiguous territories such as Darjeeling District, Sikkim and Nepal wherein they constitute an overwhelming majority of 75 per cent, over 80 per cent, and 95 per cent respectively, with a common culture, language, tradition and psychological make-up, must have the right to full autonomy in a free India so that they may freely develop further as a nationality . . . Once the major nationalities of India do justice to them, by recognising their right to freedom in a free India and once they tasted of the sweet fruit of freedom, they will undoubtedly turn into the best defends of India's freedom. The Cossacks, who were once the watch-dogs of the Czar, are now the best defenders of the freedom of the Soviet Union." (IB File No. 558/46 Part II, Ratan Lal Brahman)

The Party persisted with this line till 1947 and even beyond. For example, the CPI organised a meeting at the Market Place, Darjeeling on 8 December 1946 which was addressed by Subba and Sushil Chatterjee. They explained that the Gorkhas were a separate nation and urged to fight for Gorkhalistan, which would be in consonance with Pakistan, as demanded by the Muslim League [IB File No. 1214/42(i), Ganesh Lal Subba; extract from Abstract dated 21 December 1946, Item 5(h)]. Prof Hiren Mukherjee addressed a public meeting on 11 October 1946, at the NNHP Hall on the subject, "Development of

Gorkhas as a Nation". The meeting was organised by the CPI with a view to promoting political consciousness amongst the Gorkhas (IB File No. 810/36(i), Hirendranath Mukherjee, SL No 129, Extract Folder Pt).

On 6 April 1947, in a meeting organised by the CPI at the same venue and addressed by Bhadra Bahadur Hamal, Ratan Lal Brahman, MLA, Madan Kumar Chettri, Satyen Majumdar and Ganesh Lal Subba, when the latter read out a memorandum which was to be submitted before the Advisory Sub-Committee of the Constituent Assembly. It consisted of a number of demands, the main being for the establishment of 'Gorkhalistan' for the Gorkhas [IB File No. 558/46 Part II, Ratan Lal Brahman, Item 3(f)].

The communists carried on such activities during the war years. They could endear themselves to the British Raj, thanks to their closeness to the Muslim League. On top of it, the CPI could flourish, as the other contenders – namely, the other Left parties and the Congress – did not figure in this operation. But all this came to an end by mid-1945 with the release of the Congress leaders.

To the masses, however, the communists were a *bête-noir*. The war too had ended; so very soon they began to feel the heat.

CHAPTER FIVE

Expelled from Congress

The Second World War ended by mid-1945. Gradually, the top leadership was released from jail. Gandhi was released earlier, following his fast for 22 days. After recovering, he tried to negotiate with Jinnah in order to reach an agreement on the Hindu-Muslim problem. The Gandhi-Jinnah talks raised a lot of expectations, but in vain. An open confrontation between the two parties seemed imminent. The top political leaders of the Congress, along with those from the other parties who had participated in the Quit India Movement, were being released in mid-1945. They received a hero's welcome from the masses. Some time passed before they came to grips with the new political developments. When they realised the damage already done, they depended on their popularity and fell back on their people.

The communists were still members of the Congress, some even of the All India Congress Committee (or the AICC). They continued to pursue their policy of appeasement to the Muslim League. The result was: attack from all sides. The other Left parties – CSP, RSPI, Forward Bloc – which had taken prominent parts in the 1942 August Movement, started attacking CPI's role in the War years. Aruna Asaf Ali explained how the CPI "played an inglorious part in the '42 Movement. They misled students through their press statements. (They) threw mud at our leaders, broadcast the empty slogan of Congress-League unity" (Beware of these Communist/ Mrs Asaf Ali's Address, *The Tribune,* 12 February

1946). Soon others like Jai Prakash Narayan were to join in this campaign. Soumyendranath Tagore, leader of the Revolutionary Communist Party of India (or RCPI), started a campaign, much earlier, against the communists, through his writings – denigrating the 'Stalinists' in the War (Imperialist War to People's War/*Red Front*, March 1942; see: Tagore, Soumyendranath, *Against the Stream*: Vol. II, p.89-90).

Soli and his wife, Nargis Batlivala, were confirmed Communists. Disillusioned with the policies followed by the Party during the War, both resigned from the CPI. Later, Soli went hammers and tongs against the Party. "I challenge Joshi", thundered Soli, "to contradict me when I say that he detailed certain party members without the knowledge of the Central Committee or the rank and file of the party to be in touch with the army intelligence department and supply the CID chief with such information as they would require against nationalist workers, who were connected with the '42 Movement or against persons who had come to India on behalf of the Azad Hind Goverment of Netaji. . . . As regards the 1942 Congress Workers who carried on the struggle secretly, all party units submitted lists of such workers to the police" (Batlivala, Soli, *Facts Vs. Forgery*, p.9).

Likewise, Sardar Baldev Singh Bedi of Banga, Punjab, resigned from the District Communist Party as a protest against the 'policy of advocating the vivisection plan of the Muslim League on a plea of the right of self-determination'. In a letter covering about eighty foolscap sheets, he made scathing criticism of the Party's policy maintaining that it was 'anti-national and illogical at the present juncture when the country is passing through a crisis and national integrity is its imperative need for achieving a goal'. Other Punjabi Communist like Baba Karim Singh of Bilga and Giani Sardar Singh of Nagra, had already left the Party (Communist Party's Policy Anti-National, *The Tribune*, 26 January 1946).

On the Kishan front, the attack came from N G Ranga. ". . . We did not realise that all the fervour against Imperialism and in favour of India's freedom was only the other tactic of this party (CPI) in its attempt to alienate more and more sections of patriots from the National Congress and discredit the greatest fighters of freedom." And again, "the only lead the CPI claims to give us is that our national revolution shall go into alliance with counter-revolution and that we decide here and now to divide India before we can get India for Indians and make the bits of India the sporting ground for Imperialist rivalries between the Anglo-American and Soviet expansionists" (Ranga, N G, *Kishan and Communist*, p.11).

The communists were clearly on the defensive, yet they continued to justify their stand. At the beginning of 1945, they had, however, made certain changes in their approach. That is why the All India Students' Federation, at its meeting held in the end of 1944, directed their students not to describe the War any more as 'People's War'. This resolution as it was unanimously passed in the Conference, read: ". . . The Conference endorses the decision of the Working Committee not to characterise the war as People's War because characterisation of the war is not a burning issue facing the students, and hinders instead of helping us to the task of uniting students of all shades of opinion behind a commonly agreed policy of winning a national government to defend the country and win complete Independence for India." But it was also asserted that such modification towards the character of the War was not because Communist had lost faith in their policy; by this revised attitude, the party wanted to show their generosity towards students' unity (People's War and Students/Revision of Attitude, Amrita *Bazar Patrika*, 1 January 1945).

The communist, however, made matters worse by their persisting hate-campaign, especially against Netaji and his INA; even the General Secretary attacked Bose saying the Congressmen knew Bose as an unprincipled opportunist who had to be thrown out of the Congress (Joshi, P C, *Congress and Communist*, p.12). Bose was, however, defended by Jai Prakash Narayan, who said, "that it was easy to denounce Subhas as a Quisling....But Nationalist India knows him as a fervent patriot and as one who has always been in the forefront of his country's fight for freedom. It was inconceivable that he should ever be ready to sell his country". This attitude of the communists unavoidably isolated the party.

Netaji, by that time had become an icon of patriotism. So the disparaging remarks against the hero of the day made the communists even more isolated. In Rawalpindi, for example, the local communist workers resented such remarks. The local Congress and the CSP circles, too, were quite exasperated. A meeting on 4 August 1945, with Gurcharan Singh Khosla in the chair, attended by all prominent members of the area, passed a resolution proposed by Sriram Suri, President of the Pindi Congress Workers' Assembly. Seconded by Gurmukh Singh Puri, Secretary of the Sikh Youth League, unequivocally condemned the the communists for attacking Netaji Subhas, using objectionable words and appealed to the AICC to expel all communists from the Congress. The meeting also resolved to socially boycott communists (Communist's Disparaging Remarks Against Bose, *The Tribune*, 29 August 1945).

In the same city, a meeting of the All India Students' Congress was held a month before. Yusuf, a student leader from Kashmir, argued for an unequivocal ban on those who professed loyalty to any organisation other than the Indian National Congress. The President of the Students' Congress, R S Shukla, made a damning reference to the part the communist played in the absence of the Congress leaders. He added that the people who took instructions from a foreign country could betray their motherland's interest. They also condemned the CPI's alliance with the Muslim League (All India Students' Congress Meeting (Rawalpindi), *The Tribune*, 6 July 1945).

In Punjab, the Akalis were the principal opponent to the communists. The Sikh's case was rather different. The CPI's support to Pakistan directly affected the Sikhs, since the Akali Dal convened All India Panthic Sikhs Conference with the unity of the Sikhs in mind. So they left out the communist Sikhs, considering them obstreperous. Sardar Baldev Singh justified his anti-communist stance by arguing that no Sikh, no matter which creed or party they followed, could agree to the 'vivisection' of Punjab. As the CPI was supporting the League's demand for Pakistan, they were not invited to the Panthic Conference (Sikhs Ignored, *The Tribune*, 3 August 1945).

Again, at a conference in Jullundhar, on 22 September 1944, top Akali leaders met to criticise the CPI's slogan of Congress-Sikh-League unity, as being engendered by the selfish motive of drafting the Sikhs into the Kishan Sabha, led by the CPI. According to the Akali leaders, the simultaneous cry for Pakistan, on the one hand, and Congress-Sikh-League unity, on the other, was a mockery of national unity. At another meeting held in the city of Amritsar the Akali leaders criticised the CPI's role in popularising the demand for Pakistan (Amritsar Day By Day, *The Tribune*, 14 March 1945).

After the release of the Congress leaders, a deputation of Sikhs led by Sardar Sampuran Singh, Sardar Udham Singh and Mangat Singh met Jawaharlal Nehru. The deputation discussed the situation in Punjab. They complained that the CPI's role, in the absence of the Congress, had been despicable. They did all they could to weaken the movements launched by the Congress (Nationalist Sikhs Meets Mr Nehru, *The Tribune*, 7 July 1945).

The commoners clearly shared this view. For example, one Sailendra Nath Dutt said in the letters column of the Hindustan Standard, Calcutta, ". . . It is indeed most unfortunate that a section of so-called CPI have started a regular campaign of vilification of Congress leaders with the ostensible object of creating a split in the Congress rank and file by trying to exploit their patriotic sentiments. These CPI have been of late revolting against the Congress in every possible way and are not following Congress policy and ideology. In Bengal, a section of the CPI have been openly pleading in favour of acceptance of Jinnah's Pakistan scheme...They are going to set up League Muslims against the Nationalist Muslims in the forthcoming elections. They no longer owe allegiance to Congress but to some outside agencies . . . They have fully identified themselves with Jinnah's Pakistan scheme and its underlying policy of vivisection of India into Hindustan and Pakistan . . . Will the Congress state its attitude about these Communists who are nothing short of rank opportunists out to do mischief to the cause of India's freedom?" (Letter to the Editor by Sailendra Nath Dutt, *Hindustan Standard*, 23 September 1945).

The Congress High Command could not ignore the public mood. It also gave the Rightists within the Congress an opportunity to cleanse Congress from all Leftist influence which they had initiated at Tripuri. Bhulabhai Desai headed an enquiry committee, which was told to gather evidences against the CPI. Meanwhile, P C Joshi had entered into a series of correspondence with Gandhiji, explaining the Party's position on the People's War. The tone, on both sides, was cordial and friendly, but at the end, both agreed to differ. Thereafter, the communist members left the Congress *en masse*.

The All India Congress Committee met once again in Bombay after three years in September 1945 to take relook at the resignation, among other things.

Mian Iftikharuddin, President, Punjab Provincial Congress Committee, was a communist after all. Along with K M Ashraf, another Communist member of the AICC moved a resolution to re-negotiate with the League on accepting its demand for Pakistan. This was vehemently opposed by the other members in the AICC, with Sardar Patel pulling strings from behind. Ashraf fought a gallant battle against an overwhelming crowd that was in no mood to listen to his communist hypothesis about self-determination. Mian Iftikharuddin made the next attempt. He claimed that the League had become the 'Congress' of the Muslims. Sardar Patel argued that there could be only one Congress – not two – and Mian Iftikharuddin would be well advised to take out a membership of the Muslim League. Shortly after the AICC Session, Mian Iftikharuddin resigned from the Punjab Congress and really joined the Muslim League on 5 September 1945. The communists, continued to be still with the Congress, were show-caused – and finally expelled (Congress President Sounds Marching Orders/Unmitigated War on Muslim League, *The Tribune*, 26 September 1945, Bombay).

It now fell on P C Joshi to defend his Party and its policies. Replying to the charges levelled against his party by the Congress Working Committee, Joshi made no bones about confessing: "We support the aim of the League, as defined in its Lahore Resolution, which is nothing more than the right of sovereign freedom of the Muslims in their own homelands. We supported it for the same reason and on the same principles as we supported the Congress' aim of Purna Swaraj against the British. Just as we are against British domination over our country, we are against any Hindu domination over Muslim Homelands because of Hindu majority in India as a whole or because of the greater strength of the Hindus in every way – economic, educational and so on . . . We consider it is the Congress duty as the premier national organisation to take the initiative for building up joint front for India's freedom by accepting the principles of self-determination and guaranteeing the Muslims sovereign freedom in their own homelands and then calling upon them to give guarantees for fighting for common freedom and for defending common freedom . . . Only when the Congress guarantees the just demands of the Muslims for their own homelands can it earn the moral rights and carry confidence when it pleads common interests of India against all aggressors, which will ensure unity of effort in economic planning. And why did the Communists resign from the Congress? We called upon our party members to resign from the Congress when we read your charge-sheet and report and after we saw at the Bombay AICC what lead you instead giving the Congress, the lead of fighting the League with your back to the wall and of uprooting the Communist Party immediately" (Joshi, P C, *Communist Reply Congress Working Committee Charges*, p.235-237 and p.247). Joshi further attacked the Congress by saying, "Your propaganda that the Communists are traitors' encourages the worst of the Congressmen to bring the professional goonda into the service of the Congress and against our Party; it encourages or condones Congress boys who spread lies through whisper campaigns and manufacture the slanders which they think will turn the people against the Communist" (*Ibid*, p. 259).

So the Congress Working Committee (CWC) passed this resolution:

The CWC which met at Calcutta on 11-12 December 1945 considered the report made by the Sub-Committee consisting of Sardar Patel, Pandit Govind Ballav Pant and Jawaharlal Nehru and passed a resolution removing the Communist members of the AICC from elective bodies in the Congress. The following is the text of the CWC resolution:

The report of the Sub-Committee appointed to consider the charges brought against the Communist members of the AICC was considered and their recommendations were approved.

It is resolved that disciplinary action be taken against (1) S G Sardeasi (2) V G Bhagwat (3) V D Chitale (4) K M Ashraf (5) S Sajjad Zaheer (6) Sohan Singh Josh (7) Karyanand Sharma and (8) R D Bharadwaj, and the names be removed from membership of the AICC and from all other elective Congress Committees of which they may be members.

Further, the Provincial Congress Committees should be directed to take a similar action for the removal from all Congress elective offices of members of the CPI.

SUB-COMMITTEE REPORT

The special sub-committee appointed by the CWC (at Poona in September 1945) consisting of Sardar Vallabh Bhai Patel, Jawaharlal Nehru and Pandit Govind Ballav Pant made the following recommendations to the CWC about the Communists in the Congress: 'A large number of complaints against the activities of the Communist Party and its individual members were received by the AICC office from subordinate Congress Committees and also from some prominent Congressmen. The CWC appointed a Sub-Committee to examine the material and to take such action as might be necessary. We framed certain charges after carefully and dispassionately weighing the evidence.'

The charge-sheet was delivered to the Communist members of the AICC on 21 September 1945. They were asked to send their reply in writing within two weeks. They were also told that they could, if they so desired, see the members of the Sub-Committee and explain their position personally. On their request, a copy of the report on which the charges were based was given to them on 24 September. A letter dated 28 September was subsequently received from Sri Sardesai on their behalf asking for a week's extension to enable them to prepare the reply to the charge-sheet. This request was granted. On the expiry of the period of three weeks, another communication was received from Sri Sardesai stating that it had not been possible for them to prepare the reply within even the extended period. He definitely promised to send the same by the end of October but again failed to do so. Their reply was dispatched from Bombay about a month later on 27 November.

CHARGES NOT DENIED

The communists' explanation amounts to a tirade against the Congress. Its tone throughout is one of self-righteous arrogance. It leaves no doubt whatsoever about the validity of the charges framed against them. Clearly, they had been planning, for a considerable time, to oppose and obfuscate the policy and programme of the Congress, with the intention of undermining the prestige of the Congress in the public eye.

They thus thoroughly proved untrustworthy to the Congress and unworthy of any elective position in the Congress. Indeed, the Congress had found them out. So the Congress instructed all AICC branches to remove the members, wherever possible, of the Communist Party from all elective offices in the Congress (CWC Resolution, *Bombay Chronicle*, 13 December 1945).

Joshi hit back. Criticising, he warned that the Congress party's "declaration of fight against the Muslim League will only unleash the forces of civil war. To fortify the strength of the Congress and dent that of the League is to be blind . . . We Indian Communists consider this anti-League and anti-Communist policy of the CWC as direct encouragement to the forces of civil war which will lead to the country's ruin" (Communist Go Out of Congress/Joshi's Circular Asking

Members to Resign, *Hindustan Standard*, 16 October 1945). The Communist members of the Congress, all over the country, began to resign. Protesting against the 'anti-League' and 'anti-Communist' policy of the Congress, Z A Ahmed and other Communist members resigned from the United Provinces Congress Committee (*Morning News*, 14 September 1945).

Thus having failed to change the character of the Congress from within, the Communists broke off with the Congress. The CPI's new policy during the War years made them hugely unpopular. It had now only one option, to cling to the League and retain its popularity as much as it could by currying favour with the supporters of the Muslim League.

This betrayal of trust hung like an Albatross round the CPI's neck for a long time to come.

CHAPTER SIX

Communist Muslim League

As stated earlier, having been expelled from the Congress, the Communists had no other option but to stick to the League. Numerically it had not grown to such proportions as to launch any movement by itself. It needed to grow under the patronage of bigger parties.

Joshi did not restrict the Party to only popularising the demand for Pakistan, he even advised the Muslim Party workers to join the League. The plan was clear: infiltrate and capture the League whenever the opportunity presents itself. This 'Trojan Horse' policy of PC succeeded to certain extent when it came to the League. Some of the Communists who joined the League moved up to take up important offices within the party fold. For example, in Punjab, Daniyal Latifi, a Muslim Communist, joined the League and soon became the Office Secretary of the Punjab Provincial Muslim League and also the Office Secretary of the League Assembly Council.

A contemporary political analyst, writing in the 'Tribune', Punjab, noted sarcastically, that, "It appears that the Indian Communist Party has for some time been the training ground for prospective Muslim Leaguers. Join this great centre of intellectual chaos and learn some magic catch phrases. You are then ripe for the membership of the League" (Current Comment, *The Tribune*, 10 July 1944). Latifi, an Oxford graduate and author of the Punjab Muslim League Manifesto, wrote, 'Why I have joined Muslim League' in 1945. He also compiled the

Statistics of Pakistan (Hasan, Mushirul, *Legacy of a Divided Nation*, p.85). Similarly, the whole unit of the Student Federation was disbanded at Aligarh Muslim University and members were told to join Muslim League Students' Federation *en masse* (*Ibid*, p.113).

Before exploring the plight of the Communists within the League, let us look at a curious case of mingling Islam with Communism. Communism, being based upon the theory of dialectical materialism, preached the doctrine of Godlessness. Islam, on the other hand, was more than just a religion, even the day to day activities of its follower were guided by its tenets. Then how could such anti-theses meet? This question was raised by one Abdul Qayyum, a political worker from Punjab. "Firstly religion being an opiate of the people according to the Communist gospel should not be encouraged in any form. The whole Communist theory is against religion and considers that most of the evils of the present capitalist society are produced and sustained by religion. Recent Russian history tells us that the Communists waged a regular crusade against God and religion. There is absolutely no place for religion in their scheme for the new world order. Under the circumstances how do they reconcile their active support and encouragement of a political organisation based on religion? Do they mean to say that Marxism when applied to Indian conditions is different from what it is in Europe? Could they cite a single instance even from an authority from any great Communist leader to support their action which must otherwise, appear to be unsophisticated as a heresy" (Communists Turn Communalists/ Abdul Qayyum, *The Tribune*, 5 January 1945).

The same question was put forward by Sardar Baldev Singh, the Union Minister, in his tirade against the Communists, "To me high confidence that the Communists enjoy in the inner councils of the Muslim League everywhere is inexplicable. Mr Jinnah and his friends know this, that a number of top Muslim Leaguers are pucca Communists. That these men are spreading the poison of godlessness in Muslim homes, as accredited propagandists of the League only fools can deny. How does Mr Jinnah justify this deadly anti-Muslim drift in the high-councils of his Party?"(*Times of India*, 25 October 1945).

A question might arise: were all the Muslims who joined the Communist Party confirmed atheists? If not – how did they mix Communism with Islam? Probably they were drawn more to Socialism rather than to dialectical materialism. Socialism, albeit in a different form, already existed in Islam, so perhaps it could be taken as an ideology. To these Muslim Communists, negation of religion took a back seat and the appeal to Socialism became primary objective.

This brand of Islamic-Socialists can be traced even in the land of the Soviets. Just after the revolution, the Soviets discovered that religious beliefs die hard. So they proceeded gingerly in their propaganda against religion as far as the Muslim areas of Russia were concerned. No propagation against religion would help. The first Muslim Communists were Mulannur Vahitov and Sultan Galiev of the Kazan based Muslim Socialist Committee who campaigned for a separate Islamic Communist Party and special Muslim Units within the Russian army as well as in the local administration. These two men were involved in the creation of Communist Party's documents on National and Islamic Question. They documents consisted of:

   i) Declaration of Rights of Peoples of Russia, 1917
   ii) Address to all Muslim toilers of Russia and the East, 1917

In December 1917, under the leadership of Joseph Stalin, the Bolshevists formed the Commissariat (Ministry) of Nationalities, known as Narkomats. One of its principal departments was the Muskom or the Muslim Communists. By 1918, Galiev became the leader of the Muskom. He, in November of the same year, initiated the creation of the Central Bureau of Muslim Communists, an exclusive Muslim unit within the Russian Communist Party, and the Union of Young Muslim Socialists. The first action of this Muslim Bureau was the organisation of the First All Russian Congress of Muslim Communists which debated the issues of the separate Muslim Communist Party of Russia and the promotion of Communism among Muslims abroad.

Meanwhile, the Bolshevists had launched a campaign against the Orthodox Russian Church by a Government Decree in 1918. The idea was to spread the doctrine of atheism among the masses. But curiously, when it came to Islam and Muslims, the Party leaders and functionaries tended to refrain from making statements and comments of an offensive nature. In fact, on many public occasions, Stalin and other top Bolshevist leaders spoke favourably of Islam and the Shariat. They even stressed that there was no conflict between the Soviet system and Islam and promised the preservation of the Shariat courts in the Islamic regions of Russia. Thus the Communist regime got support from many Muslim clerics who later became to be called the red Shariatists who organised a movement with slogans like 'For Soviet power-For Shariat' (Yemelianova, Genelia M, *Russia and Islam*, p.102-03).

Even the Indian Muslims in exile, had their own contributions in popularising Communism among Soviet Muslims. Most prominent among such workers was Barkatullah, who offered his services to the Soviet Government to conduct propaganda, both in print and by words, among the former Turkish Prisoners of War who were staying in Soviet territories in the early twenties. The offer was gratefully accepted.

Barkatullah started holding conferences in Mosques, addressing his listeners as 'defenders of Islam, brothers in religion and even Comrade Muslims!' He then started publishing articles in newspapers from places like Petrograd, Alma-ata, Kazan, Samara, Taskhent, aiming at Muslim readers.

Samples of his articles published:
1) Wilson vs Lenin
2) An appeal – to all the Muslims in Asia
3) Bolshevism and Islam (pamphlet)

Here are the excerpts:

"Bolshevik ideas and the Islamic Republic had been handed down by the Lord in order to save the poor and the needy to reassure all men and bring people into kinship with each other." The document advised, ". . . To all Muslims of the world to . . .

... unite round the Soviet Government for the liberation of all oppressed subject people ..."

The Indian section of Azerbaijan Central Press Agency was set up at Baku in June 1920 for translation and publication of Soviet propaganda materials in Urdu, Hindi, Pushtu and Arabic. A fortnightly Urdu newspaper, *Azad Hindustan*, based on the principles of Islam and friendly towards Russia was also published (Persits, E M, *Revolutionaries of India in Soviet Russia*, p.167). Likewise, 'Adalat', the Tehran Underground Communist Organisation had a rule in force early in 1921, whereby anyone applying for Party membership, before full admission, had to swear on the Quran, to observe party discipline. Mustafa Nafi, a representative of the European Turkey, in a letter to the Revolutionary Military Council of Soviet Russia, on 21 February 1921, wrote, "Eastern proletariat had known about the ideas of Communism for over 13 centuries. All the Muslim saints, including Prophet Mohammed had been either peasants or workers" (*Ibid*, p.172).

Paradoxically, Islam and Communism cohabited peacefully. Out of this synthesis, a breed of workers was generated who would be pious believers in Islam and at the same time ardent preachers of the Marxian theory.

In India, the best-known name of such a worker was that of Hasrat Mohaani, a Communist who had gone to Haj thirteen times! Hasrat Mohaani was a man of all season. Previously a Congressman, a Khilafatist, he had been a Communist and finally a Muslim Leaguer. Mohaani was present in the first session of the Communist Party of India held at Kanpur 1921. He read his address as President of the Reception Committee. His address underlined the fact that as opposed to the landlords and capitalists, Communist ideology upheld the cause of workers and peasants. Islamic teachings, too, find capitalists and imperialist ideology condemnable ... The Socialist system was basically a democratic system, by no means antagonistic to Islamic principles. Mohaani declared himself a Muslim-Socialist.

In 1936, Mohaani became the President of the Kanpur branch of Progressive Writers' Association. In the same year, he joined the Muslim League, and was nominated a member of the Working Committee of the Muslim League. This post he held till 1947 and later he went on to become the staunch supporter of the Pakistan demand (Mohaani, Hasrat, *Mujaffar Hanifi* (Urdu), translated by Khadija Azeem).

Thus Communist members suffered no compunction in joining the Muslim League. The composition of the League came in for a lot of criticism. The League was dominated by landlords, nawabs, knights and feudal Lords, most of whom were staunch loyalists. How could the Communists suffer such social parasites as landlords? This was Qayyum's second question. "The poor tenants and workers who are trying to get rid of these sharks, even under the Communist's flags in UP, CP, Bengal and Bihar through the Kishan and allied organisations will have to go under if these people are put into power as a result of the Communist help. Are they not destroying the very foundations of the class struggle that they had themselves started in provinces? Even in Punjab, the Communists had succeeded in few places in their attempt to educate and organise the poor peasants against the rapacious landlords." (Communists Turn Communalists, *The Tribune*, 5 January 1945)

Similarly, Sheikh Mohammad Alam, Bar-at-Law, MLA, commented, "I must say that the Muslim Communists (if the expression is not a contradiction in terms) are neither doing justice to themselves nor to the Muslim League as both militate against a background which runs on two sets of parallel counters. They are trying to exploit each other without giving fullest scope for the fullest development and expression to each (Communism is Like a Lipstick or Scent, *The Tribune*, 22 October 1944). Curiously, no answer was provided by the Communists who hailed the League as the 'Congress' or the Nationalist force of the Muslim masses.

The League accepted the Communist offer gleefully. In the path of becoming the sole spokesman of the Muslims, there were two road-blocks, viz. the unionist coalition in Punjab and the Krishak Praja Party in Bengal, both having the support of the majority of the Muslims in those two provinces. The Unionists, a rainbow coalition of Muslim-Hindu-Sikh elites, while being loyal to the British, posed the bigger challenge. The stalwarts of the coalition, men like Sir Sikandar Hayat, Sir Fazli-Hussain and Sir Chotu Ram kept the Congress, Muslim League and the Communists at bay in Punjab. The local Communist movements such as Inqilab, Gadar, Naujawan Bharat Sabha and the Kirti Kishan Party were too weak to mount a counter, and Chotu Ram's theory of Jatt consciousness and identity was far too deeply entrenched in the Unionist Party for any Muslim leader to seriously consider Jinnah and his Muslim League. It was for nothing that Jinnah had mentioned the Punjab as the cornerstone of Pakistan.

Still Sir Sikandar thought it prudent to enter into a Sikandar-Jinnah Pact which actually benefitted the Unionists than the League. The pact fell apart in the 1940s and the League went into arms struggle against Khizar Hayat, son of Sikandar Hayat led Unionist Party.

In the opposition to the Unionists, the League needed all the support and readily got it from the Communists. The 1937 elections had proved that the League was essentially a party of the Muslim minorities in the Hindu majority provinces who demanded safe-guards. But it needed to make inroads into the Muslim majority provinces of Punjab and Bengal in order to establish its claim as the only Party looking after Muslim interests.

The Unionist's break up with the League came about after Sir Chotu Ram, the leader who succeeded the then departed Sikandar Hayat in 1944, declared that he would have nothing to do with the League and would not be dictated by Jinnah. The Unionists-League break up meant the Communist Party coming into the picture in absence of the Congress. Meanwhile, the Governor had snubbed Shaukat Hayat, the other son of Sir Sikandar and a Leaguer, for declaring that the Punjab Ministry was in effect, a League ministry. Sajjad Zaheer, the Communist, wrote, "So long as the League agreed to whatever the Unionists chose to do in its name, the Governor and his fellow bureaucrats had no objection to the Unionists being also called Muslim Leaguers. However, when it was a question of submitting to the democratic discipline of a rapidly growing people's party and of carrying out its policy and acting according to its instructions, it could not possibly be tolerated by the bureaucracy. This long brewing conflict finally came to a head in March-April 1944 . . . The last strong-hold of imperialist bureaucracy in India is invaded by the League. Let us all help the people of the Punjab to capture it" (Zaheer, Sajjad, *Light on League-Unionist Conflict*, p.26-33).

The composition of the Punjab League was more or less same as that of the Unionists, i.e. it comprised landlords and feudal heads. Daulatana and Mamdot, both zaminders, entered into an alliance with the Communists against the Unionists, who were branded as representatives of the zaminder class! (Gilmartin, David, *Empire and Islam: Punjab and the Making of Pakistan*, p.196). This alliance proved to be mutually beneficial, as it helped the Communists to increase their influence over the rural folks as Punjab was essentially a peasants' land. For the rural League leaders an alliance with the Communists helped in legitimising their position as rural leaders, independent of the Unionist ideology, and thus progressive. Also the catch-phrases of the Communists helped convincing the peasants as the League being a truly 'People's Party'.

In November 1944, the Punjab Muslim League put forward its manifesto, describing itself as a 'People's Party'. Although the manifesto was said to have been drafted by Daniyal Laifi (*Ibid*, p.196-97), it was believed to be drawn by Dr Gangadhar Adhikari, the Communist leader and touched up by none other than Mr Jinnah! (Singh, Anita Inder, *The Origin of the Partition of India*, p.128). By December 1944, the Muslim Leaguers in the province was told to associate with the Communists for joint action. The draft manifesto, according to *Punjab Tribune*, was 'wrapped up in phraseology which is popular among professed adherents of Communism', and it was unanimously adopted by Punjab Provincial Muslim League Working Committee. However, this draft would be rebuked by Khizar Hayat, who felt constrained to retort, "Yes

I know your manifesto which came to you red hot from the Communist table in Bombay" (Red Recruits in League/ Old Guard's suspicion, *Amrita Bazar Patrika*, 15 February 1945).

The Bengal situation was completely different. Here, the principal party of the Muslim masses was Krishak Praja Party with Fajlul Haq as its leader. Haq, however, in the forties made a blunder by aligning with the Hindu Mahasabha and forming the Shyama-Haq Ministry. This gave the League a chance to attack Haq. Haq became rather unpopular with the Muslim masses by this single act and the League got rid of the Ministry by courtesy of the Governor, and under Khwaja Nazimuddin, formed a League Ministry in 1943.

In Bengal League, the most prominent Islamic Socialist was Abul Hashim of Burdwan who had started his political career as a Khilafatist. Hashim graduated from Burdwan Raj College in 1928 and earned a law degree in 1931. Then he started his legal practice at the court of Burdwan. He also participated in Muslim League's Lahore conference in 1940. Later he moved onto concentrating entirely on the Muslim masses. At the same time, he was attracted to the principles of Socialism and later emerged as the most important Islamic-Socialist of his day.

Hashim first came into contact with the Communists during the fall of the Shyama-Haq Ministry in April 1943. Bankim Mukherjee, Abdur Rezzaq and Bhupesh Gupta – all Communists, discussed a document of agreement between the Muslim League and the CPI for a joint opposition to the Haq Ministry (Hashim, Abul, *In Retrospection*, p.28). The same year Hashim was made Secretary, Bengal Provincial Muslim League, maintaining close proximity with Suhrawardy. The League at that time was purely elitist in composition with groups like 1) Khwaja Nazimuddin of the Dacca Nawab family, (2) Akram Khan and his 'Azad' looking after League's publicity, (3) the House of Ispahani controlling its treasury with Suhrawardy taking a neutral ground. The biggest challenge for the new secretary was to re-organise and transform the League into a 'People's Party' with power resting with the Muslim toilers.

One evening in January 1944, Maulana Akram Khan and his son Khairul Alam took Hashim to the provincial office of the CPI. Hashim

met P C Joshi for the first time there; the leaders of the Bengal
Communist Party offered their services to Hashim in order to reorganise
League as a broad-based, democratic and progressive political party.
Hashim readily accepted the offer (*Ibid*, p.40). Thus began the
Communist-League friendship in Bengal which continued till 1947.

'Hashim wanted the Bengal League to be a bit of both of the
Congress and the CPI – a platform for all Muslim organisations, yet as
structured as the CPI. He wanted, in place of amateur workers, whole-
time cadres to constitute the nucleus of the party. He wanted party
offices in every district, and organised residences known as Party Houses
(similar to the Party Communes of the Communists). In 1944, Hashim
himself moved from his private residence to the Calcutta Party 'House-
n-Office' staying there till the end of 1946 (Calcutta Party House – 3
Wellesley 1st Lane). He instructed all units to be self-sufficient in terms
of finances and not to look at Head Quarters for aid.

Hashim took regular political classes, where he taught (Harun-or-
Rashid, *The Foreshadowing of Bangladesh: Bengal Muslim League and Muslim
Politics*, 1936-47, p.167):

- Fundamentals of Islam
- Islamic Philosophy
- Socialism
- Methods of party organisation

Hashim advised the young Party workers to consolidate and seek as
many allies as possible. When they failed to make allies, they should try
to make them neutral and thus single out the enemies and beat them in
a political battle. Hashim was successful in formally enrolling more than
half a million 2 Anna members of the Bengal Provincial Muslim League
by the end of 1944 (Hashim, Abul, *In Retrospection*, p.42, 59). The
Congress was not in the picture due to their August Movement, and
Hashim made full use of the opportunity to strengthen and spread the
Provincial Muslim League. With young people attracted to his personality,
Hashim decided to form his own party within the League. With his
knowledge of Islam and Socialism, Abul Hashim could inspire the

younger generation. In a Party House for the whole-timers in Dacca, through Hashim's patronage the principle of Islam was freely debated from the Socialist point of view. Communist methods were more or less adopted for building up the party. Under Hashim, the Communist-minded younger generation captured a majority of the seats in the Provincial Council of the Muslim League. A number of important members, with Communist leanings, infiltrated the Bengal League. They were (Ahmed, Kamruddin, *A Socio-political History of Bengal and the birth of Bangladesh*, p.61-62):

1. Abdul Haq (Jessore)
2. Mohammad Toha (Noakhali)
3. Sardar Fajlul Karim (Barishal)
4. Shamsuddin Ahmed (Secretary, Dacca Muslim League)

Abul Hashim, with help from a Communist worker, Nikhil Chakravarty, published a draft manifesto of the BPML. Published on 24 March 1945, it contained his views on what should be the ideals of the Muslim League and on the socio-economic and political objectives of Pakistan as demanded by the Muslims. The pamphlet, called 'Let Us Go to War', was widely circulated. It contained the views on the 'multi-nation' theory, as espoused by Hashim. Of course, it was based on 'two-nation' hypothesis, preached by the Muslim League. This was more or less on the CPI line of the Nationality theory. These developments were too much for the old guards to bear and they came down strongly against Hashim. They even refused to accept 'Weekly Millat' of Hashim as the organ of the League. The leadership accused the younger members in the organisation, belonging originally to the CPI, of infiltrating the League in order to capture it from within. One such accused member, Shahid Ahmed, in a letter to Nawabzada Liaqat Ali Khan, wrote, ". . . We had to start a library of Islamic books to train our boys according to the tenets of Islam at Dacca Office and made a plan to start the Quran classes for the workers, prayers had to be made compulsory". Hashim was alleged to be a Communist for the doctrine of Rabbaniyat or Islamic Socialism that he was preaching was close to Communism, and ultimately, the League old-guards refused to accept Hashim's draft being the official Manifesto as it smacked of Communistic ideas.

For all that, the bonhomie between the League and the Communists continued, and they reached an agreement on certain issues. For example, the Leftists within the League and the Communists agreed to work jointly for forging Hindu-Muslim unity on the basis of Pakistan and for the success of the impending Gandhi-Jinnah talks. They agreed also on mobilising public opinion in favour of the right of self-determination of those who were unwilling to stay within the Indian Union.

Hashim continued to influence the Muslim students by his heady mixture of Islam and Communism. On 23 June 1944, a conference of the Bengal Provincial Muslim Students' League was held at Islamia College, Calcutta, with Shamsul Haq as President. Hashim, invited to inaugurate the Conference, explained the meaning and contents of a Muslim State, with a Marxian touch and dealt at length with social and economic problems (Hashim, Abul, *In Retrospection*, p.59). Just like the Communists, Hashim tried to organise a cultural front of the League using the Muslim Sahitya Majlis for creating cultural background behind the demand of the right of self-determination for the Muslims (*Ibid*, p.54).

The Party tried to infiltrate the Muslim Students' League too. Here they found an ally in Anwar Hossain, the Secretary of the All Bengal Muslim Students' League. Already the Student Federation had come in contact with the Student League during the Bengal Famine when they created a Joint Relief Board, led by Anwar Hossain and Annada Shankar Bhattacharya, the Secretary of the Bengal Students' Federation. Later Annada sent a note to all District Secretaries of the Students' Federation saying that Anwar's happened to be the biggest and the most organised and also the most progressive group within the Muslim Students' League, and the group had the tenacity to check the growing influence of other elements in the League.

Therefore, the Students' Federation was to strengthen Anwar and the progressive section within the Students' League. Annada even instructed all hitherto unexposed Muslim contacts and comrades to move inside the Muslim Students' League to facilitate united and effective relief work on behalf of the Joint Relief Board and also to consolidate the Party's position within the Muslim Student wing. Along with this, Annada warned that any mistake from their part would jeopardise the Joint Board thus making the Muslim Students' League hostile and give a handle to the reactionaries inside the provincial Muslim League in the Working Committee of the Bengal Muslim Students' League. Another ally in the student front was Lal Mian (IB File No. 501/45, Annada Shankar Bhattacharya, Extract Folder I, p.139, 142-43).

The League leadership found the Nationality theory of the Communists quite handy. In order to vindicate their own theory that India had never been one nation, they looked for other allies who were also fighting for the same reasons. Moreover, it tried to establish that the Congress was primarily a formation of the caste-Hindus. In this, they found a natural ally in the Scheduled Castes' Federation of B R Ambedkar. Jinnah and the Muslim League leadership tried to sell the dream of a pure land where the Muslim of the subcontinent could reside and lead a life of their own. The land would be a democratic one with no exploitation whatsoever. At least in the Muslim League session held in Bombay in May 1943, Jinnah declared that he could not work for a single day if he thought that he was working for the capitalists and landlords, who fattened on the seat of the toilers. Jinnah even warned the capitalists and the landlords in the League to change with the times.

Sajjad Zaheer, a true Communist, who was present in the conference later wrote to Muzaffar Ahmed, ". . . very naturally this portion of the address was the most popular among the rank and file of the Muslim Leaguers. Talking to me they would say that Pakistan would be a socialist State and quote Mr Jinnah. I am not certain if the Nawabs, Rajas and the Knights – of whom there is abundance even in the Working Committee of the League – appreciated equally this position of Quaid-e-Azaam's speech enthusiastically. Any way, they must have been glad when Jinnah persuaded Dr Abdul Hamid Kazi and Mr Abdul Majid Sindhi to withdraw their resolutions which laid down these principles more concrete. This was, I was assured 'in the interest of Muslim solidarity" (IB File No. 168-22(i), Sajjad Zaheer to Muzaffar Ahmed, dated 4 May 1943, Part II, R1942-43, p.266-67).

In a conference held in Calcutta, on 8 October 1944, by the Council of the Calcutta Muslim League, a resolution was passed to this effect, ". . . There is a general feeling that we should try to make greater and more intense propaganda for Pakistan among (1) Depressed Class (2) the Adivasis (3) the Dravidians (4) the Kishans (5) the labourers (6) the socialists and students . . . The general belief was that failing an agreement the British would make Pakistan dependent and contingent upon the votes of the present provinces – per Cripps plan. If we have pacts with the two – the Adivasis and the Depressed Classes – we will triumph" (Pirzada, Syed Sharifuddin (Ed.), *Quaid-e-Azam Jinnah's Correspondence*, p.309). Keeping this in mind, the Bengal League encouraged Jogendranath Mandal, the leader of the Scheduled Castes' Federation in Bengal. Mandal later was to find a berth in the League Ministry in Bengal; he also joined the Interim Government as a Muslim League candidate to counter the nominations of Congress's Nationalist Muslims.

Raghib Ahsan, a Bengal League leader and editor of "Star" published from Allahabad, in a letter to Khwaja Nazimuddin, wrote, "My idea of Adivasisthan is that the Chotanagpur division and Santhal Parganas with an area of 32.592 Sq Mile and population of 97,50,846 should be formed into a separate autonomous state as a homeland of the aboriginal Adivasis . . . with East Pakistan . . . that the Pakistan state of Bengal would industrially speaking die is absolutely wrong and based on a baseless supposition and propaganda that Chaotanagpur is a Hindu-majority province . . . But Singhbhum, Bastar, Rajmahal, Jharia, and Adivasisthan area are not Hindustan and should never be allowed to be grabbed by Hindustan" (*Ibid*, p.308). The League was finding new 'Nationalities' who could strengthen their struggle against the Congress.

Khan Bahadur Maulana Mubarak Karim Sahib of Bengal Provincial Muslim League addressing a labour meeting at Kankinara (in industrial belt near Kolkata) elaborated that India had four distinct nations:

> MUSLIMS: In the North-West and East zones of India the Muslim Nation, the most democratic and socially the most homogeneous nation is in absolute majority and demanding independent Pakistan.

> DRAVIDA NAD: South of Deccan, roughly Madras Presidency, Kerala and Malabar or Dravidisthan as they can no longer tolerate the Brahmin-Bania domination of the Aryan North.

> ADIVASISTHAN: In the table-land of Chotanagpur, Santhal Parganas, Chattisgarh Mandala, Jaspur-Surguja and parts of Central Province, Orissa right up to Bastar, Kankar, Korapat and Vizag agency the Adivasi-non Aryan, Non-Hindu Aboriginal Mundari tribal are in majority and have been demanding free Adivasisthan as India's oldest Nation who peopled, civilised and ruled India long before the advent of the Vedic Aryans. The Chotanagpur Separation League, the Adivasi Mahasabha and Bhumija Mandal are the outcome of their movement for freedom. I firmly believe that no solution of the Indian political problem which fails to give full freedom and scope to this great people can be called just, democratic and permanent.

> HINDUSTAN: In the plains of Hindustan, the valley of the Ganges, Jumna, Maharastra and Gujerat, the Aryan Hindu are in a majority and are entitled to form the independent state of Hindustan with its capital at Prayag or Kashi.

The untouchables, Sikhs and Parsees etc are peoples who are in minority everywhere. Their freedom and status, therefore, can best be secured within the framework of the four majority nations states of:
- Pakistan

- Dravidistan
- Adivasisthan
- Hindustan

How far these demands were credible is debatable. But the League was flirting with such ideas primarily to put pressure on the Congress in order to emerge successful with their demand for Pakistan (Labourers Solidly Behind Muslim League, *Star of India*, 13 March 1946). The League hierarchy was happy as long as the Communists supported their cause. But once the threat of the Communists taking over the League became a possibility, the old-guards in the League became suspicious of the Communists.

The Punjab League had a number of sub-groups working together, for their own individual interests. One group was headed by Sir Feroz Khan Noon, who was a staunch loyalist and had resigned from the Viceroy's executive council to actively participate in Punjab politics (Noon later became Prime Minister of Pakistan). Nawab of Mamdot, led another group, who was also the President of the Punjab Muslim League. The third group was that of Sardar Shaukat Hayat Khan, who held sway over the minds of a certain section of the people, determined to owe allegiance to him and no one else. The fourth group comprised the Communists, Daniyal Latifi, Abdullah Malik, with Mian Iftikharuddin leading, hoping to overawe the others with their extremist programmes and slogans.

The first three groups always looked on to the last with suspicion. The new recruits coming as they did from the CPI talked of democratisation of the League and was taking it to the masses. Some of them, like Daniyal Latifi, held important positions in the Party. In order to curb the growing influence of the Communists, a move was afoot to restrict Communist or ex-Congressmen, who had joined the League to hold office (Lahore Diary, *The Civil & Military Gazette*, 22 February 1946).

In the conservative section, however, there were certain members who themselves had Communist inclinations. The General Secretary of

the Punjab League, Mumtaz Daulatana, was known to his Oxford
compatriots as a flaming 'Red'. Similarly Mumtaz Shah Nawaz, or Taazi,
daughter of Begum Shah Nawaz, the 'Sarojini Naidu' of the Punjab
League had ties with the Communists, having herself participated in
students' politics and trade unions (From Communism to
Communalism, *Bombay Chronicle Weekly*, 9 March 1947).

The conservative section of the League was, however, disturbed
by the penetration policy of the Communists in their organisation. In
their opinion, "There is no place in the League for the Communists
and Socialists and those wealthy people who want to deprive the
poor of power, simply because they are poor. The fundamental
differences between the Muslims and the Communists are due to the
fact that the Communists do not accept the Quranic conception of
spiritual and temporal values". To check the inflow of Communists,
President of the Sind Provincial Muslim League, G M Syed, and
Convenor of the sub-committee appointed by the Action
Committee of the All India Muslim League issued the following
questionnaire, seeking guidance from the Muslim thinkers and
philosophers.

The questionnaire was:

i.   Along what lines, on what basis and principles, will it be
     possible to mould, in accordance with the social, political and
     economic life of the Indian Muslims situated as they are.
ii. Suggest a workable formula, whereby different sects of
     schools of thought among the Muslims may be reconciled and
     welded together for common purpose of national renaissance.
iii. What would be the formulation of an economic plan and
     system, consistent with the Islamic principles.
iv. Bearing in mind the peculiar conditions surrounding the
     Muslims in India, will it be possible for them, if and when
     they get sovereign States in a majority of their own, to
     introduce a form of Government in which they may secure
     a happy fusion of religion and politics.

The Sub-Committee of this Committee of Action, comprised hard-liners such as G M Syed, Khaliquzzaman, Maulana Abdul Wahib, Sahib Jamal Mian of Firangi Mahal, Maulana Abdul Hamid Badauni, Maulavi Haji Ali Akbar Khan, Maulana Ghulam Murshad, Maulana Akram Khan among others, submitted a report on the feasible and appropriate steps for infusing true Islamic spirit amongst un-Islamic customs and ideas that have crept into the Muslim society (Un-Islamic Customs and Ideas, *Morning News*, 1 April 1944). Along with this, the old-guards launched a drive to expel the Communists altogether. In the month of October 1945, a resolution came up before the Provincial League Council, in the same Daulatana's name, who had himself been a Communist in his college days at Oxford, recommending expulsion of the Communists from the League. As it happened, it was not Daulatana but Raja Ghajnafar Ali who moved the resolution which was, however, not passed though (Leaguers Look Daggers at Communists, *Advance*, 21 May 1946). Similarly, a move to expel the Communists from All India Muslim Students' Federation was taken by Abdus Sattar Khan Niazi, a prominent Students' leader in the Punjab (Gilmartin, David, *Empire and Islam: Punjab and the Making of Pakistan,* p.212).

By mid-1946, another resolution demanding the expulsion of the Communists from the League was again moved by Raja Ghajnafar Ali Khan on behalf of the Punjab Muslim League Council, Lahore with the Nawab of Mamdot presiding the meeting. Ali made a scathing attack on the Communists, describing them as fifth-columnists. He branded the Communists as "the greatest enemies of Islam...assure them that their efforts to capture the League by creating disruption in its ranks will never fructify as Muslims, who implicitly believe in God, cannot be misled by any subtle technique of propaganda. Quaid-e-Azam, of all parties, singled out the Communists when he warned them to keep their hands off the Muslim League. Thus the best course for the Communists was to quit the League and return to their own organisation and thereby bring their game of divided allegiance to an end". Raja Ghajnafar Ali Khan even called upon every Muslim Leaguer to keep a strict watch on the activities of the Communists in the Muslim League.

The one leader to come to the rescue of the Communists was Mian Iftikharuddin, a known Communist sympathiser. "I shudder," Mian said, "at the very idea that the Muslim League should discuss such a resolution to expel from its ranks the most selfless and progressive workers on doubtful grounds regarding their fidelity towards Muslim League." Mian further aserted, ". . . I have full faith in the political consciousness of the Muslim public and I believe they will rather support the democratic attitude of progressive parties than commit the mistake of expelling from their ranks a group of sincere workers on grounds of unfounded suspicions". It was quite natural for Mian Iftikharuddin to act in such a manner as he was actively involved with the Friends of Soviet Union, the auxiliary unit of the CPI (Communists in Muslim League, *The Civil & Military Gazette*, 21 May 1946).

In Bengal, the target was easy. It was Abul Hashim, who had been castigated as a Communist, and was thus considered dangerous. The accusation came from people like Nazimuddin, Ispahani and Akram Khan. It was an open power struggle within the party that continued till the very end i.e. 1947. Hashim could count upon Suhrawardy, but Nazimuddin had the blessings of Nawabzada Liaqat Ali Khan, the General Secretary of All India Muslim League, who too despised men like Hashim, Ifthikharuddin and Latifi for being Communists. The rightist's point was clear: The Muslim students could and should learn the Communist philosophy of life, but they should not be Communists in thoughts and in their way of life. Any help for attaining Pakistan was welcomed but not at the expense of their own political career. In an address to the students in Calcutta, 1945, Liaqat Ali firmly asserted: "As far as the Muslim League is concerned . . . as we all know, we are fighting a struggle of life and death and those who are not with us are against us . . . I do not want to use the platform of any other party and I shall not allow my platform to be used by any other Party . . . My young friends who believe that the Communists or through Communism they will secure Pakistan, are greatly mistaken." To this Khwaja Nazimuddin would add, "I warn you against this great danger of communism to Islam. Any Muslim who is a member of the CPI and feels that he would serve better this real service by joining us will have a place with us but I do not want any Muslim to come to the Muslim League to be received with open arms and then play the part of Shivaji" (Future of India Rests with Youth/League Secretary's address, *Star of India*, 12 May 1945).

Even after such occasional threats and hint of a CPI witch-hunt, the Communists continued in the League. The hard-liners too learnt to cohabit with these 'Reds' but whenever the opportunity presented itself they tried to marginalise them. The forthcoming elections of 1946 were vitally important in order to establish the claim of being the sole spokesmen of the Muslims and to curb the influence of the Congress. To fulfil that end, the League needed the Communists and a section of the Depressed Class to pose a challenge to the Congress in the reserved seats of labour and depressed classes. Unfortunately, the Communists within the League failed dismally to provide a new orientation to the policies of the League – not to speak of Hindus and Muslims living together as a united nation.

CHAPTER SEVEN

1946 Elections

On 26 July 1945, in Britain, the Labour Party was swept to power on a landslide victory, winning just under 50 per cent of the vote, while the Conservatives' share was 36 per cent. The Labour won 393 seats – a majority of 147. The new Prime Minister, Clement Atllee, decided to go for decolonisation, starting with India. Lord Wavell, Viceroy, declared His Majesty's Government's decision to hold elections in British India in order to initiate the task of transferring power to the responsible political parties. The 1946 elections, held in eleven provinces were crucial in deciding the political destiny of South Asia. Election results not only provided constitutional answer to the question, but also hinted at the problems that the people of this region had to face after Independence.

The election gave the League an opportunity to talk to the Muslim masses and exert control over them. For the Congress, it was the occasion to prove its hegemony over the Nationalist forces in the country, which would be a step towards building up Akhand Hindustan. By the end of 1945, all political parties started gearing up for the upcoming election. Meanwhile, the British Communist Party issued a statement from London on 8 October 1945, requesting the Government to provide settlement of India's future on the following lines (Settlement of India's Future, London, *The Tribune*, 11 October 1945):

- Prepare electoral list for the whole of India based ı pon adult franchise
- Release all remaining political prisoners
- Permit establishment of temporary representative Government in provinces to supervise pre-election arrangements
- Bring into being a temporary responsible Government on the basis of Congress-League parity.

This last point made an interesting read as it demanded granting parity to the League at par with the Congress even before the League had 'earned' their right to speak on behalf of 'all' the Muslims in the country. In fact, the claim of the League being the sole spokesman of the Muslim masses was vehemently challenged by other Muslim parties. Apart from the Unionist in Punjab and Krishak Praja Party in Bengal there existed such other parties like:

- All India Majlis-e-Ahrar
- All India Momin Conference
- All India Shia Conference
- Jamat-ul-ulema-e-Hind

The Khaksars, a semi-paramilitary formation, with Allama Mashriqi as its leader.

These groups were opposed to Jinnah's Pakistan scheme, and decided to align together in order to challenge the might of the League as far as the reserved Muslim seats were concerned. Bodies like Jamat-ul-ulema-e-Hind, Momin Conference, Krishak Praja Party, the Red Shirts of Badshah Khan, the Independent Party of Bihar came together to form the Central Muslim Parliamentary Board, with Ahrars and Khaksars supporting from outside. It was, however, true that the League was the only Muslim party having an all India presence and thus was more representative.

The Ahrars and Khaksars attacked the dubious tactics of the League to alienate the Muslims from the mainstream. In a public meeting at Ludhiana, 6 October 1945, Maulana Habibur Rahman Ludhianvi, a prominent Ahrar leader commented, "India for Indians – the Congress has given lead to the country. They have decided to fight the ensuing election on 'Quit India' slogan. Muslims should not lag behind in winning freedom and I appeal to the Muslims to give their verdict in favour of 'Quit India' resolution". A mammoth crowd of 30,000 people belonging to all communities attended this meeting. Ludhianvi continued further, "I make bold to say that the Congress will capture all the Hindu seats and among the Sikh seats, the Congress will sweep the polls. Let these two factors be an eye-opener to the Muslims" (*The Tribune*, Ludhiana, 7 October 1945).

Similarly, explaining the Khaksar's stand in the elections, K L Gauba, President, Khaksar Parliamentary Board, said that the Constitution would serve as their election manifesto and anybody who would support their constitution would have their support. 'No truck with the reactionary Muslim League' – would be their election slogan. Referring to Pakistan, Gauba expressed the view that it had come to stay with the majority of the Indian Muslims as a sentiment, but the moment they came down to rationalising it, they would be disillusioned (No Truck With Reactionary League, *The Tribune*, 10 October 1945).

Jinnah targeted these Muslim groups, branding them as traitors to the cause. With a view to establishing his own hegemony over the Muslim masses, especially in Punjab, he employed the services of the clerics and ulemas to campaign for the League. In addition, Jinnah encouraged muscle power, aiming especially at the Muslim opposition. Indeed, perceiving the election to be a ploy to win Pakistan, Jinnah cared for no economic, social or political agenda.

Muslim League was evidently concerned in establishing its two-nation theory, rubbishing the Akhand Hindustan scheme of the Congress, which can be substantiated from the statement issued by Abul Hashim, with his usual Communist touch on the Nationality theory. "The Pakistan formula is very simple and corresponds with the realities of Indian politics. The basis of Pakistan is real democracy, freedom, equality and justice, and is opposed to the imperialist domination and economic exploitation which is the basis of the Akhand Hindustan scheme of the Congress. Free India was never one country. Free Indians were never one nation. Liberated India must necessarily be as God has made it, sub-continent with complete Independence for every nation inhabiting it. However, great a weakness the Congress may have for the capitalists of Bombay and how much they may desire to do them a good turn by opening to them opportunities of exploiting the whole of India under the cover of Akhand Bharat, Muslim India to a man will resist all attempts of the Congress to establish dictatorship in India of any coterie, group or organisation." (Elections Must Liquidate False Claim of Congress: Hashim, *Star of India*, 8 September 1945)

Meanwhile, the ulemas and clerics joined in League's campaign and canvassed aggressively amidst the Muslims that the time had come to choose between Din and Duniya. A vote against the League was an open invitation to the infidels to rule the roost, while strengthening the League meant helping the path of Islam. "Pakistan is a Muslim millennium and it is up to them to choose between Pakistan on the one hand or eternal servitude on the other", thundered Mufti Fakrul Islam at a meeting held in Roshan Bagh, Allahabad, on 26 September 1945, under the auspices of the Allahabad City Muslim League. Similarly speaking at a public meeting in Quetta, Baluchistan, on 18 October 1945, Jinnah himself raised this question, ". . . we want the verdict of the electorate whether they want Pakistan or whether they accept the Congress demand of Akhand Hindustan, i.e. Hindu Raj and whether Muslims want to live here as an abject minority under Hindu Raj" (No Salvation for Muslims Under the Hindu Raj: Jinnah, *Star of India*, 18 October 1945).

Similarly, Md Habibullah, Propaganda Secretary, Bengal Provincial Muslim League, published provocative leaflets targeting the Muslim voters. ". . . Islamic faith is being established in the world for equality. The sword which was used by Hazrat Mohammed, Samar Faroque, Khalique, Tarek, Musa, Md Mir Kassem, Bhaktear Khilji to conquer the world, is to be used by Islam against evils, injustice, inequality, capitalism and idolatry. This election struggle which we are contesting is a part of that war. If we are successful, Pakistan will be established in this country. We are announcing emphatically that Pakistan will establish the Government for the poor." (IB File No. 717/46, 24 Parganas, Communal tensions etc) Having thus mixed religion with politics, Jinnah developed the potential for muscling his way forward.

Bengal presented a different kettle of fish. So the League concentrated on the economic issues while facing the peasants who were mostly Muslims and densely populated in the Eastern side of the province. Here the League needed the help from the Communists, in order to present a picture of Pakistan in front of the tillers that portrayed that Pakistan meant getting rid of the zaminders, who were mostly Hindus, thanks to the Permanent Settlement.

The propaganda for the election was based on such slogans like (Harun-or-Rashid, *The Foreshadowing of Bangladesh: Bengal Muslim League and Muslim Politics, 1936-47*, p.222):

o   Land belong to the plough
o   Abolish zaminderi without compensation
o   Down with vested interests
o   Labourers will be owners
o   Pakistan for peasants and labourers

Physical assault on political opponents, especially the Nationalist Muslims, persisted. Jinnah at a meeting in Calcutta made it clear, "We are fighting the elections not to capture Ministries in the provinces but to give a decent burial to the Government of India Act, 1935, and thus establish Pakistan in the country, and that Pakistan is now a life and death question with Muslims" (Mr Jinnah's Meeting on the Maidan, *The Statesman*, 25 February 1946). Thus, no opposition, especially from the followers of the same faith, would be tolerated. Naturally, in Bengal, they targeted particularly the Muslim candidates of the Krishak Praja Party and the Congress.

One such victim was Prof Humayun Kabir, a Nationalist Muslim, being the second-in-command of the Krishak Praja Party, after Fazlul Haq. He was also a labour leader, instrumental in forming the Bengal Assam Railway Employees' Association. U N Pathak, Vice-President of the Association, in a speech before the election, recalled that Kabir's was the first voice to raise the slogan of a basic living wage for all subordinate staff, and therefore, he was chosen to contest from the reserved Railways seat. His opponent was a London-returned Communist, Jyoti Basu. Pathak commented, "Instead of joining and strengthening the long established Employees' Association, our friends of 'People's War' variety saw fit to create fresh divisions and bitterness among the workers on a most difficult period of 1942 by starting a new Union . . . It is clear that it's only objective is the Assembly elections. Faced with certain defeat, it has now resorted to vilification of all and sundry, sometimes abusing the Association, sometimes the administration and sometimes the Government for its own poor chance" (Railway Workers' Debt to Prof Kabir/Appeal for support to Prof Kabir, *Hindustan Standard*, 15 January 1946). In the electoral contest in the reserved seat of the Railways was, therefore, between Humayun Kabir and Jyoti Basu, the Communist where the League, lending whole-hearted support to the Communist, had preferred not to put up any candidate. Yet, just before the elections, Humayun Kabir was assaulted and severely injured at Bhairab Bazar Station, East Bengal, on the B A Railways by persons shouting Muslim League slogans! (Humayun Kabir Assaulted and Injured, The Tribune, 21 January 1946). Kabir ultimately lost to Jyoti Basu with just a slender margin of 8 in a tie 87 to 79 vote!

Habibur Rahman Chaudhury, President, Tippera Congress Committee, was another victim. He was contesting from the Kasba Burichang Constituency, Bengal and was kidnapped from Saldanadi Station, Comilla, while travelling by train towards Nayanpore to address an election meeting. Similar act of violence was perpetrated upon Maulana Hussain Ahmed Madani, President of the Jamait-ul-ulema-i-Hind, who was attacked and insulted by League workers at Saidpur,

Punjab. The Maulana, having a strong mass-base, however, prevented his disciples, who were present in large numbers from retaliating (League Attacks Madani, *The Tribune*, 8 October 1946).

Meanwhile, the Congress contested the elections purely on nationalist lines, appealing to the entire country to support its candidates. The party pledged Independence to the voters on 26 January 1946. Sarat Bose, campaigning for the Congress reiterated that the Congress was the only organisation that had been fighting for Independence for the last 60 years. The Congress was against Pakistan and communal organisations like the Hindu Mahasabha and the Muslim League, which, far from fighting for the Independence of the country actively co-operated with British Imperialism.

An appeal issued by the United Provinces Congress Committee read: "The Congress has decided to contest the elections to the Central and provincial assemblies, in spite of the many handicaps and obstructions placed in its way. It will enter its contest on the issue of immediate Independence of India and equal rights and opportunities for every citizen of free India. It will have for its battle-cry 'Quit India'. A chance comes to you now to show your adherence to the Indian National Congress which has become the living and vibrant symbol of India's unconquerable wish to freedom and Independence to the principle and objective of the Congress and to that well-beloved cause to which we have pledged ourselves so often." The appeal continued, "We appeal to our people to be true to this old yet ever new pledge, which has yet to be redeemed, and to remember that in the elections that are to come, individuals do not count, small groupings do not count, sectarian cries do not count – only one thing counts, the freedom and Independence of our motherland, from which all other freedoms will flow to our people" (Indians Must Vote for Congress, *The Tribune*, 22 October 1946).

In Punjab, the Panthic gathering of Sikhs declared that the Sikhs would give their hearty and full co-operation to all elements which were prepared sincerely to serve and promote the freedom, unity, integrity and welfare of India and those who were prepared to treat them as equals in the Government of the country – and not as a sub-national group. They declared, "In view of the fact that the legislatures elected in the coming elections are to form the basis for the creation of a constitution-making body, where decisions are sure to have a far reaching effect on the future of the Panth. And further, in view of the fact that the Pakistan movement, and the activities of the CPI are a grave threat to the religious, social, political and economic well-being of the Sikh community, this representative Panthic gathering, especially called for the purpose for considering the present situation relating to the general elections . . . hereby resolves that the Sikhs representatives in the Provincial and Central Legislatures should be elected and returned on the Panthic ticket, for only members representing the Sikhs and owing allegiance to the Panth can by serving the interests of the country, truly safeguard the interest of the Panth."

Master Tara Singh invited all groups and sections among the Sikhs except the CPI. Sardar Ishar Singh Majahil, General Secretary of the Shiromani Akali Dal, said that the Communists were playing into the hands of the Muslim League and were always ready to barter away the interests of the country. Any Sikh who would vote for them would prove a traitor to the Panth and the country (Sikhs to Contest Elections/ Cong-Akali Pact Likely, *Times of India*, 1 October 1945).

The Hindu Mahasabha, according to its leader Dr Gokul Chand Narang of Punjab, was compelled to contest the elections independently because of the anti-Hindu attitude of the Congress. Although the Mahasabha was with the Congress so far as their slogan of 'Quit India' was concerned, Narang opined that the Congress had all along adopted the policy of appeasement towards Muslims sacrificing the Hindus at the expense of Hindu-Muslim unity . . . The Hindu Mahasabha wanted to stand against the 'meek and weak policy' of the Congress and they were fighting the elections in order to mend the Congress. If the Congress declared unambiguously that it would never accept Pakistan under any circumstances, or it would not accept equal representation of Hindus and Muslims in the Executive Central Legislature and the Constitutional Assembly, and would not reduce the Hindu majority to a minority, there would not be any need for the Hindu Mahasabha to contest the elections. In that case the Sabha would have devoted its activities for the social alleviation of the Hindus only (Hindu Sabha Election Campaign, *The Tribune*, 18 October 1945).

On the other hand, the CPI fought the election on the basis of their Nationality Theory and the promise to obtain the right of self-determination to various nationalities. P C Joshi, in a statement outlining his Party's election programme and policy, said that the Party would contest not to expose the Congress or the League and glorify themselves, but to place a practical programme which would guarantee freedom, food and jobs for all. The CPI demanded that the future constitution-making body be based on two principles:

1) Universal Adult Suffrage
2) Sovereign Constituent Assemblies for each national areas such as Pathanland, Sind, Baluchistan, Western Muslim Punjab, Sikh Homeland for Central Punjab, Hindustan, Bihar, Rajasthan, Assam, Orissa, Andhra, Tamil Nad, Karnataka, Maharashtra, Gujerat and Bengal.

The CPI then elaborated on the line of action the Party would take in order to provide the right of self-determination for the various provinces, which were, according to the party, 'Nations' on their own.

"In case of Bengal, a prior plebiscite is to be held of both Hindu and Muslim areas to decide whether the unity of their homeland should be kept and split." This meant either Partition of Bengal or a United Bengal, but not as a part of India (Election policy of the CPI/Practical plan for freedom, *Times of India*, 15 October 1945). The other two propositions floated by the Party were for a Sikh Homeland and Vishala Andhra. "If you want to rescue one-third of your Telegu brothers and two-fifth of your land from Nizaam's gulami, to build an independent Vishala Andhra for all the Andhra people, then you must vote Communist, for our party alone has inscribed Vishala Andhra on our banner and is fighting for it." (*People's Age*, 17 March 1946) P Sundarayya, a Communist from Andhra elucidated the point: "We, Andhra Communists, want to ask, do the Andhra Congress leaders deny that we Andhras are a nation by ourselves – a people of 3 crores with a long history, our own language, our own rich cultural heritage, with common economic features and life? If they do stand for the sovereign right of the Anhidhra nation how can they oppose the same just right to the people of Sind, Baluchistan, Pathanland, West Punjab and Bengal where the Muslims form a majority of the people?" (Sundaryya, P, *Vishala Andhra*, p.73). As for Independent Andhra, the Muslims, a minority group constituting 5-10 per cent, were also promised certain safeguards regarding maintenance of the separate electorate for themselves (*ibid*, p.47).

Likewise, the Communists had plans for Sikhs as well. Gangadhar Adhikari, on his election platform of the CPI in Punjab, demanded:

a) An agreement among the Congress, League and other patriots to form a Constituent Assembly based on self-determination and justice to all national groups

b) Separate Constituent Assemblies for Punjab, the zones to be demarcated in such a way as to ensure self-determination to their representative majority areas

c) Constituencies for all Punjab States (i.e. Princely States) so that democratic governments are established.

Adhikari further provided a detailed plan for the Sikhs. The Sikhs, who numbered 51 lakhs in the whole of Punjab, were nowhere in absolute majority, except in a small contiguous patch of Firozpur and Ludhiana districts, together with Faridkot state and a part of Patiala state...the bulk of the Sikh people, i.e. 35 lakhs were dispersed in the various parts of Central Punjab, Amritsar, Jullundur, Ludhiana, Hoshiarpur with parts of Ferozpur, Lahore and Gurdaspur, Kangra, Hissar and Ambala with the states of Patiala, Faridkot, Kapurthala, Malerkotla, Nabha and Jind. This land block of central Punjab is bordered on the east by the Ambala division, with more than 76 per cent Hindu population, and on the west by the western districts of Punjab, with 74 per cent Muslims. According to the CPI plan, this area of the Central Punjab will have a separate Constituent Assembly – would be free to decide whether it becomes an autonomous unit of the Pakistan Federation or of the Hindustan Union (Adhikari, Gangadhar, *Sikh Homeland*; Jacob, T G (Ed.), *National Question in India: CPI Documents 1942-47*, p.135).

The CPI plan not only indulged in separatism, but also sowed the seed of Khalistan way back in 1940s. Many years later Comrade Harkishen Singh Surjeet admitted that the Sikh Comrades in the Party were demanding a Sikh Homeland but, that it was a tactical move to the Muslim Homeland of Pakistan, as demanded by Sajjad Zaheer and others. Joshi declared, "The League is free to plead for and get a separate sovereign Federation of Muslim majority areas living in friendly alliance with a sovereign Federation of Hindu majority areas, but not inside a common Indian Union". Joshi, however, made it clear that the CPI would help the Muslim League in the elections (Joshi, P C, *For the Final Bid for Power*, p.106).

The CPI directed the Students' Federation, the party's students' wing, to vigorously campaign for the mother organisation in the elections. Annada Shankar Bhattacharya, Secretary of the Provincial Students' Federation, sent a letter, dated 26 November 1945, to all the district students units, explaining the plan of action, which was to commence right from the school-rooms. Annada Shankar Bhattacharya writes, "To the Congress students we say: After all the Muslim students of my school or college believe in Pakistan, you think that he is misguided. But he is a student of my school of my town. So we cannot do without him. Try your best to convince him that Pakistan will mean a poor Bengal etc. This is not the way to win over the Muslim League students. Whether you like it or not, there are Communist students in every school or college . . . how do you propose to do it? By beating them? Or by arguing with them? To the League students we say: You have united the Muslim students behind the Pakistan demand. But how can you form Pakistan in Bengal if the non-Muslim students of my school (or college) oppose it?" (IB File No. 501/45, Annada Shankar Bhattacharya, Extract Folder I, p.326-27).

This stance of the CPI's supporting the League became a good enough issue for the other parties to lambast the Communists. For example, Nationalist Muslims led by Syed Ahmed Shah, President of the Indian National Muslim Association, and Chaudhuri Akbar Khan, President of the Indian Workers' Association, both in London, strongly criticised the CPI's support to the Muslim League which they described as an 'unholy alliance of Communists and Communalists'. On the other hand, S A M Qureshi, Joint Secretary of the Muslim League in London, welcomed Communists' support to the Muslim League, saying, "it would help in establishing a Soviet Pakistan". Qureshi expected a number of Muslim Communists to seek election as Muslim League candidates in the elections to follow (*Times of India*, 18 October 1945).

After expulsion from the Congress, the party once again had become isolated from mainstream politics. It thus took the policy of joining every anti-imperialist Movement that the other parties had launched. For example, the Congress students, along with the RSPI and Forward Bloc decided to observe the INA Day, demanding the release of Shahnawaz Khan, Dhillon and Gill, who were going to be court-martialled at Red Fort. All nationalist Indians were united as one man against the British: they demanded immediate release of the three Netaji's men, who had become heroes in public estimation.

The Communist Party was in a quandary: how could they participate in such an agitation whom they had dubbed as fifth-columnist and traitors during the War years? Therefore, when the Provincial Secretary directed the entire Students' Federation to agitate on "Release and relief of INA men" the question naturally came up: what about the controversy they themselves had created by criticising Bose as the 'lap dog of Jap-Imperialism'? The Secretary had also cautioned his comrades, "in your agitation you need not say that they were misguided etc. We opposed these men when they tried to invade India in collaboration with the Japs. Today Jap Fascists are crushed and the INA does not exist. So, we want them to join Indian freedom movement too in the future" (IB File No. 501/45, Annada Shankar Bhattacharya, Extract Folder I, 19 November 1945, p.325). Sadly for them, such a stance was perceived as opportunism and nothing else.

Coming back to the elections, the League's policy could be well-understood: it wanted to minimise the power of the Congress even in non-Muslim constituencies. For that they used the Scheduled Castes' Federation, which was opposed to the Congress, and like the League, viewed the Congress as a Brahmin-Baniya-Caste-Hindu formation. It also touted the idea that the Scheduled Castes or the Adivasis did not belong to the Hindu community. This theme had its advantage, as the Hindus without the Scheduled Caste community would fail to retain its majority status in a number of districts, naturally the Pakistan demand would gain in strength.

The League, on its part, needed the Communists to provide an intellectual sugar-coating to a demand that was basically communal. Moreover, it minimised the Communists' challenge in the labour seats. Thus the Parliamentary Board of Punjab Provincial Muslim League decided not to issue any directive concerning the three labour seats of Punjab Assembly.

In Bengal, however, the case was rather different. Here Hashim had warned the Communists beforehand that friendly relation between the League and the Communists would suffer if there was any contest between the League and the Communist candidate in any of the Muslim constituencies. Hashim assured the CPI of the League's support in the reserved labour seats. But the CPI disagreed, arguing that they had some influence in the Muslim-dominated areas, where they will surely succeed. Hence, they put up their candidates at Noakhali and Mymensingh. All the same, the CPI candidates were defeated, forfeiting their security deposits. In terms of their commitment, although the League supported the CPI in the labour constituencies, the CPI's unpopularity was in evidence from its failure in the so-called bastion, which left a mark on the relationship between the League and the Communists.

Look now at the position of the CPI in the Muslim Seats which was as follows:

Communist Candidates:	2
Elected:	0
Votes polled:	3,244
Percentage of total votes cast in favour of CPI:	0.13

(Hashim, Abul, *In Retrospection*, p.101-02)

In the non-Muslim seats, campaigning was not easy, especially when the top leaderships of the Congress looked daggers at the Communist. Sardar Patel was a known adversary, but even Jawaharlal Nehru, a self-proclaimed 'Leftist' started attacking the Communists. "Supposing a miracle occurs and Mr Jinnah's dream crystallises, India will then have a Pakistan in the east and a Pakistan in the west with the blood of the Muslim masses there being constantly sucked by the religious-capitalists and feudal parasites. Will this spectacle please Indian CPI?" (Pt Nehru on Unity of India, *The Tribune*, 13 July 1945).

The electoral battle was not restricted to verbal abuse only; soon it degenerated into physical assault. The pandal of the conference arranged by the CPI controlled local Mazdur Committee, at Sargodha, Punjab, was the scene of a pandemonium, when on the second night of the Conference, Comrade Rachpal Singh of Lyallpur, spoke against the Congress and its policies. The raising of anti-Communist slogans by a group of young men served as a signal for the public to get up, cut the ropes holding the shamiana and burn the CPI Red Flag (Red Flag Burnt by Angry Crowd, *The Tribune*, 19 October 1945).

Similarly, a meeting of the CPI held at Monghyr, Bihar, which was addressed by P C Joshi had to be abandoned because of persistent cat-calls and anti-Communist slogans raised by a large number of anti-Communist demonstrators (*The Pioneer*, 14 February 1946). Joshi was, however, not to be perturbed by such incidents. Speaking in a meeting held in Jessore, East Bengal, he gleefully declared, ". . . 25 years ago our elders worked for Hindu-Muslim Unity. Now we are the only persons working for it. We have united both Hindus and Muslims on the same platform in our mass organisation. The Congress could not have such Muslim gatherings nor does the League have as many Hindus as we have". He continued saying the CPI was the first to carry the banner of freedom to the untouchables, Kishans, workers, fishermen and all other sections of the rural population, the real proletariat (Communist Alone Work for Unity, *The Pioneer*, 23 January 1946). The Party Secretary failed to realise that his Party's idea of Hindu-Muslim unity which was based only upon the acceptance of Pakistan, was actually divisive.

In the run up to the elections, physical attacks continued; this time it was the CPI headquarters at Khetwadi, Bombay where the infuriated mob smashed the office furniture, set all the books and papers on fire and seriously damaged the printing press of the *People's Age*, the central organ of the Party. The provocation seemed to be from some disparaging remarks on Netaji by certain Communist workers. Gangadhar Adhikari, editor of the *People's Age*, said, "We are sure that no Congressmen would like to honour the memory of his leaders by committing acts of hooliganism against brother Indians" (Mob Raids Communist Party Office, *The Statesman*, 26 January 1946). This particular incident was condemned by the Congress leadership, especially Nehru. "It is not enough to say that the members of the CPI have made themselves unpopular with their anti-national policies and activities. I know that I am convinced that they have injured our national cause as well as themselves. But are people to misbehave for this reason and injure our cause still further? The Congress must dissociate itself from this completely and Congressmen must see to it that their fair name is not strained" (Pt Nehru Condemns Attacks, *The Statesman*, 27 January 1946). The Congress, however, for the first time crossed sword with the Communist in the Bombay Municipal Corporation bye-election causing the death of B Parelkar. Congress candidate V B Karagaonkar was opposed by Communist contender R K Bhogle (*The Tribune*, 27 October 1945).

The election related violence continued to escalate, in the general and labour seats between the Congress and the Communist workers, especially in Bengal. Relationship will be strained, percolating to families, between Congressite fathers and Communist sons. In Bihar, for example, Nripen Bannerjee, a sitting Congress Assembly member, faced stiff opposition in the election from his own son Sunil Bannerjee, Secretary, Bihar Communist Party, in their home constituency of Monghyr. Similarly, Ramcharitter Singh, another Congress MLA, was opposed by his son, Chandrasekhar, a Communist, in their constituency of Beguserai (Sons to Oppose Their Fathers' Bihar Assembly Election, *Morning News*, 28 November 1945).

In the electoral alliance, the Communists had decided to support the Muslim League candidates against nationalist Muslims; the League too returned the favour in the labour seats. But convincing the voters was not an easy task. During the election campaign in Kanpur, the Communists were asked to explain their conduct in the 1942 Movement, when the nation rose in revolt against British Imperialism. One such incident occurred at the gates of the Government G&S Factory, when a Communist leader from Bombay attempted to address a few workers on launching a struggle against the employers (Where Were You in 1942? Workers Poser to Communist, *National Herald*, 23 January 1946).

In Kanpur, the situation sharply deteriorated on the polling days. On 12 March 1946, rioting broke out in several places in Kanpur. At one stage the situation became so tense that police opened fire twice to disperse crowds, two persons being killed and six injured. Hindu-Muslim relations had already been strained as a result of the Congress supporting the candidature of Abdul Qayyum, a Nationalist Muslim, who opposed the Muslim League candidate, Hasrat Mohaani, in the Kanpur (Cawnpore) Muslim Urban constituency.

On the same day, i.e. 12 March 1946, shouting slogans of the rival parties started the trouble. Polling at one of the booths had to be suspended in the morning. As the trouble spread, there was a big decline in voting. The CPI gave full support to Piarelal Talib, the candidate of the Scheduled Castes' Federation, against the Congress candidates, Jawaharlal Rohatgi and Bhagwan Din Mehta. Reports of trucks flying with League flag helped to carry Scheduled Caste voters to the polling booths appeared on the newspapers (Elections Lead to Riots in Cawnpore/Police Fire on Unruly Mobs, Arson and Stray Assaults, *Times of India*, 13 March 1946).

Similar incidents occurred in Calcutta. Over half-a-dozen persons were injured when Congressmen and certain workers, allegedly Communists, came to clash on Potter Road (eastern side of the city) on 11 March 1946. The situation worsened the following morning owing to an unprovoked attack on two persons of the locality by the CPI workers; but the Congress workers intervened and peace was restored. In another incident on 18 March 1946, when a procession of the local Congressmen was passing near the Kamarhati Jute Mills, a clash ensued with a number of persons, alleged to be loyal to the CPI. Eight persons received severe injuries (Calcutta Fracas/Communist Attack on Congressmen, *Times of India*, 13 March 1946). In yet another incident on 24 March, at Bally Jute Mill, which was a labour seat, 200 persons were injured. Towards the close of polling, a band of CPI supporters threatened the voters in one of the booths. This led to an altercation between the supporters of Sibnath Banerjee, the Congress candidate who was a labour leader and Bankim Mukherjee, the Communist candidate. Later one of the groups was alleged to have attacked others with lathis and other weapons. During the melee, a dozen Congress volunteers were severely injured. Another Congress worker, who was on duty at the polling booth, was reported to be missing after the incident. The poll violence spread to other places in quick succession. Nearly 50 persons, most of them were Congress workers, received injuries in front of polling booths at Metiaburz, in the Kidderpore area. The office of 'Pratyaha', a Bengali daily newspaper of Calcutta, situated near the CPI party office in Bow Bazar Street was raided by a gang of miscreants, wearing red caps and shouting Communist slogans, reported the Joint Editor of the daily (Bengal Election Disorders, *Times of India*, 19 March 1946).

In the industrial (unorganised) labour constituency of Lucknow (plus Allahabad plus Agra plus Aligarh) the polling for B K Mukherjee, the Congress candidate, was brisk and he was reported to have secured over 80 per cent of the total votes polled. The Communist candidate, Z A Ahmed, had very little chance. In 1945, Z A Ahmed resigned from the United Provinces Congress Committee, protesting the anti-League and anti-Communist policies of the Congress. More than 7,000 voters exercised their right of franchise. The Muslim League had joined the Communists but their 'combination failed to break the solidarity of the workers', commented the Newspaper reports. In Allahabad, the CPI again combined with the Muslim League and Scheduled Castes Federation, which, however, did not make any impact. In many quarters, where the CPI claimed to have much influence, the workers, however, refused to support Z A Ahmed. Much later, some Communists confessed that it was really difficult to convince the workers in that particular election. It seemed that the workers had their own slogans:

Roti ke liye Lal Jhanda, Raaj ke liye Congress

In Aligarh, out of the total 750 voters about 500 exercised their right. Mukherjee was estimated to have polled at least 400 votes, despite the Muslim League's co-operation with Z A Ahmed.

In Kanpur, the contest was confined between Raja Ram Shastri of Congress and S S Yusuf of the CPI. It was estimated that 41,000 voters, out of the total of 72,000, exercised their right of franchise, with about 31,000 voting for the Congress candidate. The votes that were cast for the Communist candidate were not so much pro-Communist. The Muslim League entered into an alliance with the CPI against the Congress, banking on communal feelings. Some of the officials also showed a distinct bias towards the Communist candidate. The Muslim League, actively working for the Communist candidate, said that though they did not agree with the policy of the CPI, yet they were helping their candidates only to demonstrate their opposition to the Congress. Having received active support of the Muslim Leaguers, the Communist candidate Sant Singh Yusuf, styled himself as Maulana Yusuf, was almost sure to win the Muslim workers in his favour. But all his manoeuvres failed, as the workers voted overwhelmingly for the Congress (Congress

Candidates Sweep Polls/Elections in UP Assembly for Labour Seat, *National Herald*, 26 March 1946).

The CPI was trounced in the general constituencies in the UP, in desperation had joined hands with the Muslim League, thus stirring up communal bitterness. This was the allegation of Jagan Prasad Rawat, Secretary, United Provinces Congress Committee, after the elections, who stated, "In the last Assembly elections, the Communists have been beaten in all parts of the country, and with the exception of a few individuals practically every Communist candidate had his security forfeited. In raising the cry of Pakistan, Indian Communist candidates have stooped low, enough to join the communal organisation and have their best to create communal bitterness" (Betrayal Charge on Communists, *National Herald*, 16 April 1946).

The CPI, indeed, looked like supporting the Congress off and on but did so with the ulterior motive of helping the League. For example, the Delhi Provincial Communist Party appealed to the Muslims in Delhi to vote for Asaf Ali of the Congress for Central Assembly. "The CPI does recognise the fact that in the present phase of Congress-League relations, a joint electorate seat creates a difficult situation for the Muslims electors who are overwhelming for Pakistan and Muslim League. But the Party wants the Muslims to see that the real contest in Delhi is between the Congress and Hindu Mahasabha and not between the Congress and the League. Today every position of vantage captured by the Mahasabha from the Congress makes the chances of Congress-League unity and the realisation of Muslim self-determination a remote possibility. Ultimately, the Congress and the League and not the Hindu Mahasabha and the League will have to unite for realisation of our common aim – freedom for all. That is free Hindustan and free Pakistan" (Vote for Asaf Ali: Communist Plea, *Times of India*, 20 November 1945).

The poll violence between the Congress and the Communist gladdened the Imperial Government. It felt happy, "considering the bitterness with which the elections were fought in some Muslim constituencies between the League and its opponents and in labour constituencies between the Communist and the Congress labour candidates". The official dispatch said, "the contest between the Congress and the Communist for the labour and some rural seats produced more trouble than the fight between League and other Muslims. The labour and other constituencies where Communist challenged the Congress, the voting public have voted overwhelmingly for the Congress" (Kamala Sarkar, *Bengal Politics*, p.238). The resentment of the nationalist forces against the Communist would continue even after the elections. For example, in April 1946, The Federation of Indian Students Societies in London disaffiliated itself from the AISF. At the request of a majority of its students, Rafiq Zakaria, President of London Majlis, said, "most of the student organisations in Britain were against the Communistic policies of AISF" (Kick for Indian Communist, *Advance*, 14 April 1946).

Prior to the Elections, the Congress had been in the wilderness for more than three years, its organisation had broken down and many of its leaders were still behind bars and Party fund had been sequestrated by the Government (Begum, Jahanara, *The Last Decade of Undivided Bengal*, p.153). But the poll result showed that for the majority of Indians, Congress was still the vanguard of anti-Imperialist struggle. On the other hand, the Muslim League, who in 1937 had secured only 4.8 per cent of the total Muslim votes, got 76 per cent in 1946.

1946 Elections-Muslim League	League	Opposition
Bombay	5,200	310
UP	20,470	6,710
Madras	8,672	761
Punjab	8,553	1,801
Bihar	1,235	249
Assam	4,497	697
Sind	17,165	7,887
Bengal	67,230	3,719
NWFP	5,883	8,159
TOTAL	1,38,905	30,293

In Punjab, the League polled 65.10 per cent of the Muslim votes. In Bengal, it was even better, 83.6 per cent. The Krishak Praja Party secured barely 5.3 per cent, thus becoming irrelevant, and some of its members crossed over to the Muslim League. The CPI's result was dismal, winning three seats in Bengal, one in Bombay and one in the Central Assembly, secured by Somnath Lahiri. The Congress emerged as the principal Nationalist party in the general and labour seats. In Bengal, the Scheduled Caste Federation could win only one seat, while the Congress Scheduled Caste candidates won 26 seats and three seats were won by the Independents. Nevertheless, the League projected Jogen Mandal, the sole wining Scheduled Castes' Federation candidate as the spokesman of the entire Scheduled Caste community, and made him the Judicial Minster in the Muslim League Government led by Suhrawardy.

The following tables show the Party positions:

General Constituencies: Bengal Provincial Assembly

Party	Contested	Seats Won	Votes Polled	% of Voting
Congress	74	71	21,68,801	75.2%
Communist	11	1	1,18,936	4.1%
MUSLIM CONSTITUENCIES				
Muslim				
League	117	110	20,36,049	83.6%
Congress	06	00	1,759	0.5%
Krishak Praja	44	04	1,31,191	5.3%
Communist	2	00	3,244	0.12%
ALL CONSTITUENCIES				
Congress	98	86	23,34,812	42.12%
Muslim League	122	11	4,20,86,775	36.75%
Hindu Mahasabha	28	1	79,187	1.43%
Krishak Praja	44	04	1,31,191	5.3%
Communist	24	03	1,59,304	2.87%
Scheduled Castes' Federation	08	01	97,604	1.75%

(Begum, Jahanara, *The Last Decade of Undivided Bengal*, p.196)

The figures stated above are important as they reflect which way the public opinion was tilted. In general seats, if the Congress ruled the roost, it fared dismally in the Muslim reserved seats, securing only 0.5% of the Muslim votes while the League, with 83.6% just outplayed both the Congress and KPP. Fajlul Haq's party lost its glamour of 1937. By 1945, most of the top leaders of KPP like Abdul Mansur Ahmed, Abdull-el-Baqui, Shamsuddin Ahmed (Secretary, KPP), Hasan Ali, Nurul Islam Chowdhury and Giasuddin Ahmed had joined the League (*Ibid*, 152). Although Hindu Mahasabha won only one seat, that too by Shyama Prasad Mukherjee who came back unopposed, the Mahasabha could successfully mould Hindu sentiments subsequently in the province! On the other hand, Scheduled Castes' Federation won only one seat securing just 1.75 per cent of the votes, but the Federation, courtesy Muslim League, was to be portrayed as the custodian of Scheduled Caste interest in the province!

The Communists too, fared badly. They could win only 3 seats with all their heavy-weights losing. After the election debacle, it was time for stock-taking. In Bengal, the Party think-tank was divided into two camps. One was led by Bhupesh Gupta and Kumud Biswas who, in the inner-party meeting, asserted that the party policy vis-à-vis self-determination was all wrong, that the party was victim of Pakistan deviations. Bhupesh Gupta suggested opposing Pakistan, calling the League communal and propagandising self-determination of Natural National Units. He noted, "It is necessary to realise how their (League) leadership is diverting their urges to wrong and patriotic channels . . .". "Larke Lenge Pakistan" is being fast transferred into a hymn of hate, directed against the Hindus and the Congress. He went to the extent of asserting, "while we must rouse all the patriotic passions of the people, let us not invent patriotism where there exists none. I say this because very often we call a life-long League leader, patriot. A first rate scoundrel may remain in commanding position in a popular organisation if only for the time being" (IB File No. 865/46, Searches on CPI office, Bhupesh Gupta, Notes of discussion, p.334).

The other group, led by Bankim Mukherjee and Prof Hiren Mukherjee, thought that the "Natural National Unit" was of course an ideal thing but at present it was out of the picture, and the Party must recognise something like "Muslim a Nation". All India Muslim solidarity was a progressive reality and therefore, two sub-federation by splitting Bengal and Punjab was just a demand. Curiously, Joshi criticised both the opinions saying the former was a line of 'tailism' to the Congress and the latter was a line of 'tailism' to League. What he instead suggested was a revised draft on self-determination where the link between the just Muslim demand and the self-determination of natural national units was to be shown (IB File No. 865/46, Searches on CPI office, p.339).

In an extended Provincial Committee meeting held on 27 May 1946, Bhawani Sen analysed the poll results. Sen viewed, "General Hindu people believe firmly that we are supporters of Jinnah's Pakistan; Muslims who support us believe that CPI supports Pakistan of Jinnah; that is why we get support of Muslim masses in working class areas and failed to get votes where we set our candidates against the League". As to the votes polled for CPI, Sen commented, "Only in Chittagong, we got Bhadralok votes".

Thus, the new line propounded by Bhawani Sen was,

"Our agitation: move with caution
Don't go against Pakistan straight: Explain patiently
We should say – Muslim League is the biggest mass organisation
of Muslims

What we should do: is to campaign inside League for: democratic solution of the problem and common demand with Congress against British. We should have done fractional work in League: this must be done now" (IB File No. 865/46, Searches at CPI offices in Calcutta and other places on 16 September 1946; Bhawani Sen's final reporting to extended Provincial Committee, dated 29 May 1946, p.333).

The elections were over. And the League got the mandate to speak on behalf of Muslim India. Its adversary was as usual the Congress. Now both waited for the Award to be granted by His Majesty's Government.

CHAPTER EIGHT

Mission and Rajani Palme Dutt

The elections of 1946 decided as to which parties the power would be transferred to. At the beginning of the year, a delegation of British Parliamentarians, comprising Lord Chorley, Sorensen, Nicholson and others visited India and held interviews with the local leaders. They returned to England and shared their opinions with the Government. After completion of the elections, the Government decided to send another 'three member delegation' to formulate a solution to the Indian problem. This was to be called the Cabinet Mission, with Lord Pethic-Lawrence, Secretary of State for India, Sir Stafford Cripps, President of the Board of Trade and A V Alexander, First Lord of Admiralty, as the three wise men, assisted by Lord Wavell, the Viceroy.

Shortly after their return to England, Sorensen, in an interview, expressed his view on the Indian situation. He held that the Muslims had been greatly roused by this Pakistan slogan, and were not bothered about its rationality . . . "It has become more than a mere literary aspiration – great emotional spirit is generated behind it. It has reached a pitch of great excitement. In the great Muslim cities of Calcutta and North West Frontier there is great excitement about Pakistan, but when you study Mr Jinnah's scheme of Pakistan, it becomes clearer that it will be extremely difficult and impossible for Pakistan to exist as a separate state. The problem is capable of solution if only this emotion swayed away a bit and pro-Pakistan Muslims are convinced that India really is a unit" (First Thing We Can Do Is To Quit India: Sorensen, *Bombay Chronicle*, 14 March 1946).

The Cabinet Mission reached India on 24 March 1946. At a press conference, just after their arrival, the Mission made its intentions clear: "We have come with only one fixed intention, and that is to play full part as representing HMG in helping Indians to achieve their Independence. Beyond that we have open minds and are not committed to any particular views . . ." (Smooth and Peaceful Transfer of Power: Cabinet Mission, *Bombay Chronicle*, 26 March 1946).

Meanwhile, the relation between the two leading parties had deteriorated further after the elections. Muslim League had emerged as the principal party but had secured a little less than the number of seats required to form a Ministry of its own. At this juncture, the Unionists, led by Khizar, entered into an understanding with the Congress and the Akalis, and a coalition ministry was formed.

The League became furious, with Liaqat Ali issuing a stern warning, "It is a mistaken idea that a Quisling Muslim will be able to dominate Punjab Muslims with the support of the non-Muslim groups. Similarly, it will be a blunder on the part of the Hindus and the Sikhs if they coalesce for the formation of a Ministry with a party which had absolutely no public support. If in these circumstances the Governor calls upon Malik Khizar Hayat to form a Ministry, he is either misinformed or dishonest" (Liaqat Ali: *Bombay Chronicle*, 7 March 1946). With such developments in the background, the task of reaching a consensus solution was indeed a tough mission.

By the end of March, 1946, the Labour Government gave permission to Rajani Palme Dutt to visit India and cover the Cabinet Mission proceedings as a special correspondent of 'Daily Worker'. This visit was to be historical for Palme-Dutt as he had never visited India before. He was born at Cambridge in 1896, where his father, Upendra Krishna Dutt, came from India in 1875 and practised as a surgeon. His mother, Anna Palme Dutt was Swedish. She was related to the future Prime Minister of Sweden Olof Palme. Rajani Palme-Dutt, as a student, was quite meritorious, but was expelled from Oxford University, where he was a Balliol Scholar, winning first-class honours in 1917, for his 'Socialist' propaganda during the Great War. He had joined the CPGB in 1920 and in 1921 founded a monthly magazine called *Labour Monthly*, a publication which he edited until his death. Internationally, he was known for his books and writing as one of the foremost English speaking exponents of Marxism, and after the expulsion of M N Roy, Palme was the man who controlled and directed the Indian Communist Party.

Meanwhile, the Cabinet Mission continued its task of meeting leaders of the various political parties and imbibing feedbacks. The Mission told Jinnah that if he insisted on a fully sovereign Pakistan, it would have to be on the truncated variety, excluding most of Assam and half of Bengal and Punjab. Another alternative was put to him by the Mission, a proposal of three-tier Constitution – Provinces, Groups or Sub-Federation of Provinces, and a Union. Under this, the Groups of Provinces that he claimed for Pakistan would have a large measure of autonomy and would be joined with the rest in the Union, confined to the control of Defence, Foreign Affairs and Communications. It was further indicated that in the all-India Union, the Hindu and Muslim majority groups would have the right to secede from the Union after a period of 10 years (Moon, Penderel (Ed.), *Cabinet Mission: Opening Discussions Wavell: The Viceroy's Journal*, p.226).

The British, while advocating a united India, always held the Balkanisation of the Indian Sub-Continent as their Plan B. It had its variations. In fact, all major offers coming from the Government during and Post-World War had Balkanisation, hidden between lines, starting from the Cripps Mission, 1942:

"His Majesty's Government undertakes to accept and implement forthwith the Constitution so framed subject only to:

The right of any province of British India that is not prepared to accept the new Constitution to retain its present Constitutional position, provision being made for its subsequent accession if it so decides.

With such non-acceding Provinces, should they so desire, HMG would be prepared to agree upon a new Constitution giving them full status as the Indian Union which Ram Manohar Lohia analysed as, "India is to be split into four Indias (Lohia, Ram Manohar, *The Mystery of Sir Stafford Cripps*, p.19):

1. India of such British Indian Provinces which choose 'to retain its present constitutional position'
2. The India of such non-acceding provinces which decide to form a Union of their own
3. The India of Princely States which may not elect to adhere to the Constitution
4. The dismembered rest of India to form the Indian Union.

Likewise, the Cabinet Mission came up with their 16 May offer, which envisaged a United India, keeping in mind the Congress and Muslim League aspirations. But, the idea of having groupings of Muslim majority provinces (one in the western side and another in the east comprising Bengal and Assam) and Hindu majority provinces and balancing both at the Central Legislature was opposed by the Congress. This plan was to be called the Long Term Plan. The League found a provision for Pakistan in these Groupings and thus could not accept any changes made as the balance or 'parity' which was unacceptable to the Congress and which formed the basis of Muslim demand of 'political safeguards'. The second alternative put forward by the Mission was the formation of an Interim Government or the Short-term plan, which the Congress reluctantly accepted. This, eventually, came to be followed by the League.

While the Mission was busy formulating this Award, Lord Wavell unfolded his 'Breakdown Plan' to the members, with the 'Big Stick' note as a post script. The breakdown was nothing but a "policy of immediate withdrawal of our authority, influence and power from India, unconditionally, would, to my mind, be disastrous and even more fatal to the traditions and morale of our people and to our position in the world than a policy of repression . . . If we are forced into the extreme position, we should hand over the Hindu Provinces, by agreements and as peacefully as possible, to Hindu rule, withdrawing troops, officials and nationals in an orderly manner, and should at the same time support the Muslim Provinces of India against Hindu domination and assist them to work out their own constitution . . ." (Wavell: *Appendix IV: Lord Wavell's Appreciation of Possibilities in India, 30-05-46*, p.485)

If this Plan of the Viceroy were carried out, it would have spelled chaos and a dreadful civil war resulting in the Balkanisation of the sub-Continent. Thankfully, this proposal was rejected by the Mission, but Cripps came up with something that was equally unacceptable. The Mission proposed that the Princely States should regain Independence when the British left India – a proposal which, 'rather shocked the Secretary of State'. Even later, Lord Temple-Wood, former Secretary of State for India, in May 1947, opined, "As things are at present drifting, I cannot see how fragmentation of India – some would call it Balkanisation of India – can be avoided. If and when this fragmentation of India comes about, let us at least make it clear that we shall welcome any parts of India that still wish to remain within the Commonwealth will be absolutely free to adopt its own methods, politics and institutions".

The balkanisation plan would not be shelved for long. The last Viceroy, Lord Mountbatten, would re-open it again with his 'Plan Balkan'. This was to be presented to the Governor's Conference on 15 April 1947. This envisaged the transfer of power to Provinces, or to such confederation of Provinces as might decide to group together, before the actual transfer of power. It initiated the division of India into separate areas of control for the Indian National Congress, Muslim League and the Princely States. In a note dated 11 May 1947, Nehru indicated displeasure with this Plan (Singh, Anita Inder, *The Origin of the Partition of India*, p.227).

Alan Campbell-Johnson, who witnessed these proceedings, later noted, ". . . the breakdown seems to him (Nehru) to amount to little less than connivance at Balkanisation. He really wants it to be fully established that India and the Constituent Assembly are the successors to, and Pakistan and the Muslim League the seceders from, British India" (Campbell-Jonson, Alan, *Mission with Mountbatten*, p.89). Thus an amended 'Plan Balkan' with an Appendix drafted by V P Menon was offered and agreed by Nehru which made clear that the transfer of power would only be granted to two successor dominions with referenda in the NWFP and Bengal to decide between Hindustan and Pakistan, which was named 'Plan Partition'.

While interviewing the members of the Muslim League, for some reason, the Cabinet Mission seemed to think that 'the Muslim League had joined with the Communists'. (Wavell: Page 230) Finally, the Mission interviewed P C Joshi on 17 April 1946. Joshi submitted a memorandum stating the Communist solution of the Indian problem. The memo suggested the establishment of a Provisional Government based on the main popular parties and said that the best course would be an agreement between the Congress and the League for parity (which Congress opposed) and an adequate representation of minorities. "We suggest that the Provisional Government should be charged with the task of setting up a boundaries commission to redraw the boundaries on the basis of natural, ancient homelands of every people, so that re-demarcated provinces become as far as possible linguistically and culturally homogenous national units, for example, Sind, Pathanland in West Punjab. The people of each unit should have the unfettered right of self-determination – that is, the right to decide freely whether they would join the Indian Union or form a separate, sovereign state or another Indian Union. The election to the Constituent Assembly, should therefore, be based on the recognition of the fundamental right and during the elections the question of separation or union should be put by the political parties to the people. The delegates elected from each national unit should decide by a majority whether they will join the all-India Constituent Assembly to form an Indian Union or remain out and form a separate state by themselves or join another Indian Union" (Units Must Have the Right to Secede: Joshi's Memorandum to the Cabinet Mission, *The Pioneer*, 18 April 1946). As it surfaced, the proposals would only encourage other separatist groups on the plea of the nationality theory at a time when the entire nation was passing through a turmoil charged with communal hatred.

Meanwhile, Rajani Palme Dutt had landed in India. For the first time he was to meet most of his Indian disciples, the ones whom he had guided and compassed through turbulent times. He knew well that he too had his share in formulating the strategies of the CPI in regard to Pakistan on the basis of the nationality theory. He was also aware of the mood of the Nationalist and other Left forces. About a year before, Jawaharlal Nehru had written to him on this subject. "You must realise," Nehru said, "that it pains me to see the gulf that has arisen between the Congress and the Communist . . . that has got nothing to do with Communism and Socialism, in favour of which there is considerable though rather vague sentiment. The gulf has arisen because of internal policy in India and the fact that Communist ran down popular leaders in India, and at a time when there was bitter conflict between nationalism and the imperialist structure, they appeared before the people as acting on the side of the latter (but this policy was CPGB's brainchild) . . . They have become full-blooded supporters of Jinnah's demand (unspecified and vague as they are) and in the name of Congress-League unity, they demand a complete surrender by Congress to Jinnah. The Communists who have joined the Muslim League appear to be more rabid Leaguers than the others. All this has been greatly resented." (Nehru to RPD, Gulmarg, 12 August 1945)

Palme-Dutt must have been aware of this fact. He asked Sardar Patel if he could explain the position to the Congress on the right of self-determination, including the right of secession from any territorial unit. Patel gave his own opinion: he thought, if the League felt that the Congress was acting as a drawback on the Muslim community then the Congress was prepared to agree to a redistribution of the province in such a manner as to allow them the fullest possible autonomy in the areas in which they were in predominant majority, provided they agreed to a common policy in matters of common interests. The Congress would not agree at all to the Partition of India for the simple reason that this would harm the interests of both the communities. In that case the borders would be unsafe vis-à-vis the bigger powers. Young India, with freedom attained, must not face an uncertain future. Once the agreement was reached, the Congress would honour it, and would be loath to coerce any of the constituents to remain in the Union against wishes of its people. But this separatist attitude is unfortunate because it is predicated on the notion that the two communities cannot live together. So it would of course go round convincing people that such a notion is false. (Patel Explains Meaning of Self-determination/Reply to RPD's Question on Pakistan, *National Herald*, 1 April 1946).

Dutt quickly realised that a patch up with the Congress was necessary in order to return to mainstream politics. At the same time, opposition to the League was becoming untenable. Dutt decided to act diplomatically and advised the Indian Communists to follow the same. The advice to his disciples was: "build up the broken bridges with the Congress. The difference between the CPI and the Congress over the character of the War would become a thing of the past but support to the Muslim League's demand of Pakistan was the real hindrance" (RPD and Indian Communist: P C Joshi in New Thinking Communists, 1 March 2001, see: Chakravarty, Gargi, *P C Joshi*). Answering reporters' questions, Dutt said: "It was not true to say that the CPI was working in collusion with the League. What the Communists had done was to try to understand the nature of the Muslim mass movement . . . The problem of Pakistan can be approached from a democratic standpoint . . . the will of the people in these areas was clearly established by universal suffrage or plebiscite or some such democratic means" (Transfer of Power to India/ Dutt's Emphasis on Terms, *Amrita Bazar Patrika*, 12 April 1946).

It was, however, not easy for the CPI anymore to distance itself from the Pakistan movement. Over the years, the idea of Pakistan had taken a definite shape and the Communists had their share in popularising the demand. Dutt now advised the CPI to keep a neutral appearance; urging unity in conformity with the demand of the Congress but not altogether rejecting the demand for Pakistan (Moitra, Kiran, *Roy Comintern and Marxism in India*, p.227). The alternative was to support the Pakistan movement but criticise the 'top-reactionary' leadership of the League. Some of Dutt's Indian comrades were not happy about his article in *Labour Monthly*, March 1946, named, "India and Pakistan", wherein he had identified the League as a communal organisation. Bhupesh Gupta later noted, ". . . Some Comrades seem, rather bitter against RPD for using the expression 'communal' in connection with the Muslim League . . . Since the expression is understood in a bad sense, we SHOULD NOT (emphasis in original) use it in regard to Muslim League . . . Pakistan is the freedom urge of the Muslim masses (IB File No. 865/46, Searches of CPI offices in Calcutta and other places on 16 September 1946, p.335). The Communists were to support Pakistan through their theory of nationalities. Answering the press at Bezwada, Dutt clarified, "Indian Communists take the Muslim League as one of the patriotic parties in India. What the Indian Communists say is to recognise that the Muslims give their support to the League and it is no use dubbing all of them as reactionaries and coming in the way of the country's freedom. There is real mass expression behind the Muslim League. There is no room for confusion on this matter". He added, "I do not accept the two-nation theory of the Muslim League. I say it is wrong. The CPI's proposal consists of the theory of 17 national groups on a fully voluntary basis. This is a reasonable approach to the problem, and there need not be a Partition of India. The Communist programme was altogether different from the reactionary programme of the Muslim League and its two-Nation theory" (RPD on League and Communist, *National Herald*, 26 May 1946).

It was, however, too late. The Pakistan idea had become part of the psyche of most of the Muslims. Though the CPI started criticising the leadership of the League, they could not quite extricate themselves from their policy of appeasement to the League. The CPI had become a prisoner of the past. Indeed, subsequent events show that they continued their support to the League's movements.

The Congress, in terms of the June Award of the Cabinet Mission, decided to join the Interim Government. The League later followed suit.

But Nehru made a blunder before that.

CHAPTER NINE

Direct Action

Jawaharlal Nehru succeeded Maulana Azad as Congress President in July 1946. At the very first press conference he held, Nehru quite boldly asserted, "What we do in the Constituent Assembly we are entirely and absolutely free to determine. We would never accept any dictation or any directive from the British Government" (India Will Tear Up Any Treaty If Imposed by Britain: Nehru, *Bombay Chronicle*, 11 July 1946). This statement was enough provocation for the Muslim League, which was already unhappy with the representation ratio in the Interim Government, to reject the offer of the Cabinet Mission – both the terms of the Congress and the interim proposals of the Mission. The Working Committee of the Muslim League sat at the end of July 1946 in Bombay and discussed the then situation with the Congress President's statement in mind.

It protested on two counts:

1) Reversal of the Viceroy's Council, without reference to the League, and of the ratio of representation in the proposed Interim Government – from 5 Congress, 5 Muslim League and 2 minorities to 6 Congress, 5 Muslim League and 3 minorities, and

2) Failure of the British Government to clear the confusion caused by the Congress interpretation regarding a) groupings of

provinces and (b) status of the Constituent Assembly and thus reassuring the Muslim League.

It stressed that it was actually the groupings that contained the 'germs of Pakistan', and was essentially a part of the long term proposals, without which all that the Muslim League has stood for would be nullified. The Working Committee then contended that it would not take any responsibility for the betrayal of trust by the League which should have gone by what it had already accepted. The League thereafter gave a call to its members to give up all titles bestowed upon them by the Government, end constitutionalism, and resort to Direct Action (League for Total Rejection on British Plan: *Bombay Chronicle*, 29 July 1946).

Most members of the Muslim League Council believed that the Congress and the Government had joined hands to strangle the aspirations of the Muslim Nation. Some of the statements issued were quite intimidating. Sir Ghulam Hidayatullah, the Sind Premier, deplored the fact that the Congress had turned down all attempts of the Muslim League to accommodate rival claims ... "The Congress should understand that unless they make friends with us and accede to our demands, there will be no peace in India." Maulana Abdul Haye endorsed the plea for immediate Direct Action and said, "The Congress is out to annihilate us and the British Government is at the back of the Congress. Muslims are prepared to make all sacrifice that is demanded of them".

Sir Feroz Khan Noon went a step further and threatened, "havoc that the Muslims would play would put to shame what Changez Khan and Halaku did". Khwaja Nazimuddin of Bengal hinted, "there are 101 ways in which we can create difficulties, especially when we are not restricted to non-violence. The Moslem population of Bengal knows very well what Direct Action would mean and so we need not bother to give them any lead". Maulana Burhamul Haq expressed the conviction that the line for compromise had passed. He also asserted that the Congress was out to eradicate the Muslims in alliance with the British

Government and stressed the need for shedding their blood in vindicating their honour and safeguarding their interests.

Hasan A Sheikh, Secretary, Bombay Muslim League, opined, "By denying Mr Jinnah the monopoly of nominating all the Muslims in the Interim Government, Lord Pethick Lawrence had repudiated the representative character of the Muslim League. If the Muslim League decided to stay out of the Constituent Assembly, the only alternative before them would be to embark upon immediate Action" (League Council Meeting: Jinnah Ask for Clear Mandate, *National Herald*, 30 July 1946).

There were some rational outpourings as well. Mian Iftikharuddin, former President of Punjab Provincial Congress Committee, and a Communist fellow-traveller, who was for the first time joining the Muslim League, got an opportunity to speak in the Muslim League Council. He expressed a much more restrained view and said that for the last seven years he had been indulging in propaganda for the League in the Congress; but his efforts were abortive. "Now I will voice my appeal from this platform to the leaders of the Congress to accept the hands of co-operation extended by the Muslim League. In accepting the Cabinet Mission proposals, the Muslim League had given up its demand for a sovereign Pakistan state and it was up to the Congress to reciprocate the gesture." He added that the Congress wanted freedom neither for the country nor for the Muslims. As the biggest political organisation in the country, the major responsibility for a settlement rested on the Congress. The Muslim League had proffered its hands of co-operation to the Congress, unfortunately it was refused. Iftikharuddin then offered a solution. The long-term proposals of the Cabinet delegates should be changed into an agreement between the Muslim League and the Congress, whereby the Congress should in the first hand recognise the representative character of the Muslim League and secondly allow the 'B' and 'C' groups to consolidate themselves for the betterment of each other. "If you do not acquiesce in our demands of Pakistan, then agree upon this temporary compromise." Unless the Congress agreed to work hand in hand with the Muslim

League, the constitutional problem of India would never be solved. Lastly, he assured that the Direct Action would be free from communal tinge. "Our slogan will be revolution and not communal riots."

The next sane voice in the League Council came from Abul Hashim. "If the Muslims have to launch a struggle, let it not be against the Hindus. Our slogan must be revolution and not communal riots or civil war. The Muslims will have to fight against the Government whether it is the British or the Congress. But they would not want to kill innocent women and children because they happen to be Hindus"...Such forewarnings were to turn prophetic. Hashim advised that Muslims should resist the attempts of the Congress in the name of freedom and liberty to dominate over the Muslims. Their objective was Pakistan which meant the elimination of British Imperialism. Abul Hashim's statement was historical but it failed to cut through the hardliners. This was perhaps the tragedy of Muslim politics in the sub-continent, that emotion always held sway over rationalism. The rationalists in the League were cut to size by the fanatics. Syed Ali Akbar Shah of Sind opposed the speech made by Mian Iftikharuddin and said that no useful purpose would be served by patching up with the Congress. He urged that in embarking on any course of action, the Muslim League should never lose sight of the principles of Islam. Whatever decisions the League takes it should be in strict conformity with what is laid down in the Quran. Unfortunately, the League, in its Direct Action programme, stuck to this line. Another saner voice of Qadiruddin, President of Delhi Provincial Muslim League, who pointed out that in India civil war was impracticable, that violence would result only in communal riots, was discarded. This added to the misery of the common public who were to suffer from the orgy of blood-shed that followed.

Finally, it was the turn of the Qaid-e-Azam. Jinnah declared, "What we have done today is the most historic act in our history. Never have we in the whole history of the Muslim League done anything except by constitutional methods and by constitutionalism. But now we are obliged and forced into this position. This day we bid goodbye to constitutional methods." (League Council Goes Back On Delhi Decision:

Bombay Chronicle, 30 July 1946) This came from a man who had left the Congress because the organisation, under Gandhi, had become more radical and did not coalesce with his 'constitutional' nature. But Jinnah had to prove his point to all and sundry that without the League no solution could be found, that the League had its teeth and could bite. The rest could interpret the decision as they wished. And history would show how it could go violent with H S Suhrawardy at the helm.

INTERLUDE

To counter the war-cry of the League, the Congress and other nationalist forces joined together to celebrate 9 August Day on a grand scale, especially in Calcutta. 9 August 1946 was a Friday preceding 16 August. Makhan Pal, Secretary, RSP, Bengal Committee, issued a statement on 7 August appealing to all nationalist forces to forge together to make the day a success. "Four years ago in 1942, the final struggle for ending imperialist strangle-hold on India was started by the Indian masses under the slogan of 'Quit India'. In the context of the post-war period, the August Day of this year assumes new historical significance and in potent with new revolutionary possibilities. I, therefore, appeal to all anti-imperialist organisations in the province and especially to all workers, peasants, students, employees in offices and other establishment, artisans and shop-keepers, to join in the celebration 'en masse' and to make it an all-round success. All units of RSPI in Bengal are hereby directed to co-operate with the Congress and other anti-imperialist organisations in the August Day celebration" (4th August Revolution Day: RSPI Appeal, *Hindustan Standard*, 8 August 1946).

The organisations (alphabetically arranged) that participated in making the day a success in Calcutta were:

- Azad Hind Dal
- Bangiya Chhatra Parishad
- Bharat Mangal Samiti
- Bharat Seva Dal
- Calcutta University Students' Union

- Congress Sahitya Sangha
- Congress Socialist Party
- Forward Bloc
- Hindustan Seva Dal
- INA Relief Committee
- Indian National Congress
- Jatiya Mahila Sangha
- RSPI

These organisations celebrated the day with processions, *prabhat-feries*, hoisting National Flag, with patriotic songs and a condolence meeting, with the pledge taken to win freedom. The day passed off peacefully, as no clashes were reported. The Communists were left out of the celebration of the August Day, as they had opposed it since 1942. Instead, they welcomed the Muslim League's call for 'Direct Action' hailing it as 'anti-imperialist sentiment of the Muslim masses' (League Decision Welcomed: *Times of India*, 1 August 1946).

The CPI issued a statement recording its appreciation of the urge and desire of the Muslim masses to fight Imperialism and its new plan'. P C Joshi viewed, "the League resolution must come as an eye-opener to the Congress leadership. All their plans based on the constitution-making body will be blown up if the League persists in its rejection". Further, Joshi advised the Congress leadership to learn a lesson from this: reject the British plan and build a joint struggle with the Muslim League against the British refusal to quit India on the slogan of Constituent Assembly based on adult franchise and self-determination (League Decision on Indian Plan: P C Joshi's Retort to Congress, *Star of India*, 1 August 1946).

Some say, it would have been more prudent of the Congress, especially Nehru, to refrain from issuing any provocative statement, and start a dialogue with the League for an understanding on the question of 'parity'. Nehru could have accepted both the ideas, for the long term – groupings, and for the short term – Interim Government. The Nationalist Muslims, whose numbers had already dwindled, could have been persuaded to take a back seat for a while. The alternative to this was chaos, culminating into a civil-war, or the inevitable Partition.

The Muslim League had attained power primarily by way of playing with the emotions of the masses. They successfully sold the idea of Pakistan as the only solution to all the woes of the Muslims. Some demands of the Muslims were of course just, but unfortunately they were tinged with communal frenzy, and its communalism that the League banked on. It seems that the future and other economic prospects of Pakistan were hardly important to be discussed. Still later, it would be proved that religion alone can never be the pre-condition for the formation of a modern State. It could at best generate high-strung emotional melodrama.

PREPARATIONS

Saheed Suhrawardy, the Bengal Premier, whom Lord Wavell, the Viceroy had once described as, "the most inefficient, conceited and crooked politician in India", declared 16 August 1946, the Direct Action Day, as a public holiday in the province. This, he said, was based on the Negotiable Instrument's Act for the purpose of minimising the risks of conflict and in the interest of peace and order. On 5 August, under the *nom-de-plume* of 'Shaheed', Suhrawardy wrote an article in *The Statesman*, Calcutta, in which he reminded, "Bloodshed and disorder are not necessarily evils in themselves if resorted to for a noble cause. Among Muslims today, no cause is dearer or nobler than Pakistan" (*The Statesman*, Calcutta, 5 August 1946). This declaration of public holiday sent signals to the Hindus that something sinister was cooking underneath and they, apparently in response to the Hindu Mahasabha, started consolidating themselves. In North Calcutta, the various body-building clubs and *akharas* guarded the localities, fully armed. The preparations had begun.

The Bengal Congress stormed out of the Bengal Legislative Assembly on 12 August afternoon, after making a noisy scene. The House was full of confusion when, following the refusal of the Deputy

Speaker to admit an adjournment motion tabled on behalf of the Congress Party, continued to read a statement of his in spite of shouting and table-thumping from the Muslim League benches. The House was adjourned for 15 minutes to find a way out of the imbroglio but to no avail (Congress Members Walk-Out of Bengal Assembly, *Advance*, 13 August 1946). It was a withdrawal of the entire Opposition minus the three Communist MLAs. The Congress, subsequently held a meeting at Deshapriya Park on 14 August, protested against the arbitrary order of the League Ministry to call a Holiday on 16 August.

Meanwhile, the Bengal Provincial Muslim League started a vigorous campaign to make the Direct Action Day a grand success. Workers were told to congregate at the foot of Ochterlony Monument after offering their Jumma Prayers. It specifically appealed to the Muslim toilers to participate in large numbers. At the end of the Joint Conference of the Executive Committee of the Calcutta District and City Muslim League, many labour leaders and *mohulla sardars* declared observance of a complete hartal – that is, they went on a general strike. Leaders of seamen, and workers of inland and seagoing streamers, docks, customs, Port Trust, companies, firms, hotels, transport services, buses, trams, trains announced that they would join the hartal and meeting. Faiz Ahmed, General Secretary of the Indian Seamen's Union declared, "No seamen shall attend the Shipping Office and the offices of the Shipping Companies for any work on 16 August. A procession of the seamen will be led from the Union Head Office at Kidderpore to Ochterlony Monument" (Complete Hartal on August 16: *Star of India*, 9 August 1946). Abdul Khalik Chowdhury, Secretary, All India Streamer Employees' Muslim League, appealed to the streamer services employees all over India, "16 August is a memorable day for all Muslims. The All India Muslim League has declared the above day as the 'Direct Action' Day. Observe the day by completely absenting yourself from work and joining the mass rally at the Maidan. They will not tolerate it any more. Remember that the success of Direct Action Day depends on every individual amongst you". The Directive was: (a) After Jumma Prayers on 16 August, all streamer services men will gather at the office of the League at 15 Blochman Street, Calcutta, and (b) from this place, the procession will proceed to the Maidan (Steamer Workers to Join General Strike, *Star of India*, 10 August 1946).

Similarly, Nurul Huda, Vice-President, All India Railway Muslim Employees' Association, announced, "Let there be meetings and peaceful demonstrations on this momentous 16 August in every branch of our organisation throughout India, to voice the feeling of the Muslim Nation" (Observe Direct Action Day: Call to Railway Muslim Staff, *Star of India*, 14 August 1946).

Where they did not have much influence, the Muslim League requested the unions of other parties to support their Direct Action Day programme. S M Usmani, Secretary, Calcutta and District Muslim League, addressed a letter to the Secretary, Bus Syndicate, which was controlled by M N Roy's Union, Indian Federation of Labour, asking him to observe a hartal on 16 August . . . "We appeal to your Syndicate to observe a complete Bus hartal on 16 August . . . It should be noted that your Syndicate, which claims to represent all classes of motor bus businessmen, has always observed hartals on previous occasions at the call of the Congress organisation, and the Muslims have joined your strike without obstruction. It is but fair that you should not obstruct this anti-imperialist all-India strike and fully cooperate with us in making this strike complete. We seek sincerely your co-operation and hope that you will not make any discrimination between the Congress and the Muslim League" (Appeal to Bus Syndicate to Observe Direct Action: *The Statesman*, 15 August 1946). Rajani Mukherjee, Secretary of the Syndicate, on the contrary, issued a statement saying, "The Indian Federation of Labour and its constituent units will not associate themselves in the observance of Direct Action Day. If any Trade Union were to do so, it would spell disaster for the labour movement". He urged the Muslim League to desist from bringing pressure on labour to join the demonstration by abstaining from work as 'this is likely to split labour into rival communal camps and destroy its solidarity" (Rajani Mukherjee's Statement, *The Statesman*, 15 August 1946).

The non-League Trade Union that did join the League's programme was the CPI-controlled Tramway Workers' Union. The workers of this Union had a four hour session at the University Institute Hall, with Comrade Mohd Ismail presiding. During the 1946 election campaign at Raipur, Central Provinces, the same Mohd Ismail had drawn the mass attention to the Pakistan demand of the League and had explained the stance of his party (CPI) vis-à-vis the League demand. He had supported the Pakistan demand then saying that it was the natural outcome of the freedom urge of the Muslims, and had pointed out that it was in the interest of the country that different people were allowed to develop their policy according to their culture. Now, under him, the Communist Tram Workers' Union decided to stage a one day strike on 16 August to 'maintain the solidarity of the workers' in their fight against British Imperialism'. Somnath Lahiri and Dhiren Majumdar were also present in this meeting (Tramways Not to Work Tomorrow, *The Statesman*, 15 August 1946). Apart from the Tram Workers' Union, the CPI controlled Union in Oriental Gas Company, Belur, National Iron and Steel Workers' Union, and Bally Chatkal Workers' Union too decided to support the Muslim League. On top of these, the CPI and its Bengali organ 'Swadhinata' joined the Direct Action Day and decided 'as an act of solidarity' to keep their office closed for that day (*Swadhinata*, 16 August 1946).

CHERUBIM AND SERAPHIM

Apart from the unions, the Muslim League also called on other anti-Imperialist organisations to join the Direct Action Day. "In view of the fact that Muslims have generally joined the previous strikes which have been organised by the other parties in the cause of freedom, we do hope and trust that these parties will also join the League struggle against Imperialist-fascist forces. The Muslim League's fight is a holy war on tyranny, caste-domination, capitalist exploitation and fascist tendencies manifest in India. The League stands for the equal freedom and security of the Muslims and Hindus, the Scheduled Castes and the Adivasis as also for the economic and social emancipation of the workers and peasants." (The Complete Hartal on 16 August/Programme for Direct Action/Appeal to Other Parties, *Star of India*, 9 August 1946)

In another statement issued by the Calcutta District Muslim League, the League invited, "Representatives of minorities, suppressed and oppressed people and anti-fascist parties who have been unjustly bypassed by the British Government and who are ready to make a common cause with the League in its fight for the equal freedom of the Muslims, the Hindus, the Scheduled Castes, the Adivasis, the tribals, the Christians and other people are welcome in the meeting. The League is pledged to fight all caste prejudices, racial hatred, capitalist evils and imperialist exploitations and we call upon all other fighters for right, liberty and justice, brotherhood and equality to stand by the righteous fight of the Muslim League" (Direct Action Day in Calcutta: The Statement of the Calcutta District Muslim League, *Star of India*, 10 August 1946).

These statements were made for the world to judge the League as an alternative anti-imperialist platform of all the exploited groups. To the common Muslims, the call was, however, based upon aggressive religious lines. It was directed more against the Hindus who had allied with the British to strangle the Muslim Nation's aspirations. Excerpts from the 'Programme of Direct Action Day' by Calcutta District Muslim League suggest: "Muslims must remember that it was during Ramzan that the Quran was revealed. It was in Ramzan that the permission of Jehad was granted by Allah. It was in Ramzan that the Battle of Badr, the first open conflict between Islam and Heathenism was fought and won by 313 Muslims and again it was in the Ramzan that 10,000 Muslims under the Holy Prophet conquered Mecca and established the Kingdom of Heaven and the commonwealth of Islam in Arabia. The Muslim League is fortunate that it is starting its action in this holy month." (Programme for Direct Action, *Star of India*, 13 August 1946)

Likewise, in an Urdu circular issued by the Calcutta District Muslim League on the eve of Direct Action, the community asked itself to, "proclaim to the world at large that the Muslims are awake, that they are a brave people and that they are determined to secure their freedom. Let the blind see, the deaf hear and dumb speak out that the Muslims are a living nation and will not rest till freedom is achieved . . . Let them exhibit their action that they are ready to sacrifice themselves like Sirajodoulla, Syed Ahmed Barelvi, Tipu Sultan and that they are prepared to be annihilated rather than be slaves of the British and the Hindu and that they will not rest until India is freed from British domination and Brahmin-Bania grip. The time has come when you are called upon to lay down your lives in the final battle for freedom and God willing this will lead to the establishment of the Great Muslim state of which Pakistan will be a cornerstone" (An Urdu circular issued by the CDML on the eve of Direct Action, Das, Suranjan, *et al, Caste and Communal Politics in South Asia*, p.199).

Apart from the Communists, the Scheduled Castes' Federation participated in the League's programme. It declared on 14 August 1946 that the Federation shall observe general strike with the League. The League targeted this organisation in particular to make Hindu society vulnerable, as without the Scheduled Castes, the Hindus would lose majority in a number of districts in Bengal. So the League looked upon Scheduled Castes' Federation as a non-Hindu organisation. However, the Caste-Hindu politicians considered this to be a sheer act of opportunism. The League treated Jogen Mandal, the Federation leader in Bengal, as the leader of all Scheduled Castes in Bengal, although his Party had performed dismally in the 1946 Elections. Out of 30 seats in the reserved Scheduled Castes Constituencies, the Federation won only one, with Mandal himself winning, but the Congress won 26 Scheduled Castes, the rest having gone to the independents. Nevertheless, Mandal became the Judicial Minister in the Suhrawardy Ministry; he was a minister in the earlier Nazimuddin Ministry as well.

Ambedkar, Mandal's mentor, however, attacked the Cabinet Mission for not inviting him to the Interim Government as the representative of all Scheduled Castes. In a meeting, he described the Cabinet Mission's proposals for the future constitution of India to be an 'atom bomb' of sorts to the Scheduled Castes, who had not been recognised as a separate entity. The Federation resorted to Poona Satyagraha demanding separate safeguards for eight crores Scheduled Castes. On 15 August, just a day before the League's Direct Action, Schedule Castes' Federation celebrated the Poona Satyagraha Day, at the foot of Ochterlony Monument, the same venue that was to be used by the League on the following day. The League was quick to lend its support to the demands of the Federation. Usmani, the Secretary of Calcutta and District Muslim League issued a statement describing the Poona Pact had put over 70 million Scheduled Castes under perpetual serfdom of the caste-Hindus, and the Muslims whole-heartedly supported the rights of the Schedule Castes for separate electorates which was one condition for their emancipation. All Mussalmans were directed to stand by their Schedule Caste brothers and adivasis, whom the British deprived in order to appease the caste-Hindu Congress (Anti-Poona Pact Day, *Star of India*, 14 August 1946). And at the beginning of 1946, the CPI participated in the League-sponsored Rashid Day! Of course there was nothing new in the CPI joining a League-sponsored programme.

At the end of the War, when the INA surrendered to the Allied forces, the British Government decided to initiate a trial for Netaji's men. By then, the news of Netaji and his men had reached India. The Nationalist Indians were shocked beyond measure. Subhas Chandra was a national hero, who had immensely influenced the nationalists – including the Congress and Gandhi. Public opinion wanted the release of INA soldiers: Shahnawaz, Dhillon and Sehgal. The Nationalist forces celebrated the INA Day, and it soon ended up in street fighting between police forces of the Raj and the nationalists. The CPI, who had called during the War, Netaji and his men "traitors" and "fifth-columnists", saw in it an opportunity for returning to the mainstream. And believe it or not, they supported the agitation.

The League, too, could not just stand aloof and watch. But they needed an organisation that supported their cause of a separate Muslim

Nation, and who, even while joining a nationalist outfit like the INA, must at the same time agreed to separatism. Fortunately, they found one in Captain Abdul Rashid of the INA!

Captain Abdul Rashid, charged in the 4th INA trial, created a sensation in the courtroom, when reading from a written statement declared: "I was cut off from the world and could get only such news as were supplied by the Japs. I was convinced that the non-Muslims who were the moving spirits in the INA were going to invade India with the help of the Japs. In order to safeguard the interests of my community, I decided, like most of the other Muslims, to join the INA, in order to arm myself and thus be in a position to safeguard the interests of my community in India" (Joined INA to Protect Muslim Interest, *Star of India*, 26 January 1946). Meanwhile, Major Shahnawaz was hailed as a hero, a nationalist Muslim, someone to be emulated. The League, naturally despised this idea, and even taunted Shahnawaz as 'Pandit.' Rashid was to become the 'hero' of the Muslim League.

Jinnah took up the case of Rashid, and issued a statement pointing out that there was a great deal of resentment and tremendous stir among the Muslims. This concerned the discrimination that had been shown in commuting the sentence of Captain Rashid of the INA to seven years whereas Shahnawaz, Sehgal and Dhillon were left off completely. He called upon the Commander in Chief to explain and give his reasons and grounds for such discrimination. Otherwise, Jinnah said that the Muslims would have no option but to resort to agitation (Mr Jinnah Asks C-in-C to Explain, *Star of India*, 7 February 1946).

The student wing of the Bengal League, announced the observation of the Captain Rashid Day on Saturday 9 February 1946. Moazzam Ahmed Chaudhury, Secretary, Calcutta Muslim Students' League, declared a general strike of the students of Calcutta in protest against the conviction of Captain Rashid. They appealed to all political organisations to join the demonstrations against the act of the Government (Students Declare Strike on 9 February, *Star of India*, 7 February 1946). The nationalist Indians were reluctant to join forces with the League's demand because of its communal overtone, although the latter protested against police excesses (Stark Discrimination, *Star of India*, 9 February, 1946).

The CPI and its students' wing, the AISF, participated in observing Rashid Day, hailing it as 'an anti-Imperialist expression' of the Muslim masses. The street fight that followed was intense. Four days of stringent martial law was required to bring Calcutta back to normal. But by then nearly 50 were dead and over five hundred injured. About 60 participants, mostly students, were rounded up and later produced before the Chief Presidency Magistrate's Court. Out of them, 13 were released unconditionally. Chowdhury Moazzam Hossain or Lal Mian of the League and Bhupesh Gupta of the CPI were present in the court on behalf of the Calcutta Firing Relief and Legal Defence Committee, which were jointly formed by the League and the CPI. Sushil Sen and Kazi Nazmul Haq respectively representing the City Students' Federation and All India Muslim Students' League were also present. The released students were then taken to the City League Office amidst loud cheers (Echo of Calcutta Disturbances, 13 Students Released, *Morning News*, 19 February 1946).

So expectedly the CPI joined the League's programme of Direct Action. But they did so very tactfully as Rajani Palme-Dutt had advised them to distance themselves from the League, with a view to returning to the mainstream of Indian politics. Hence, the party joined Direct Action in a low key – as an act of solidarity with the Muslims.

Jyoti Basu, the Communist leader in the Assembly, issued a statement on behalf of the party, "We recognise that the Muslim masses, as distinct from the Muslim League leaders, have taken the League resolution as a call for mass action against the British power in India. During the last few months, the remarkable anti-Imperialist upsurge of the Muslim masses has shown itself in their common and fighting stand...But the League leadership does have no such fighting spirit. They are only being worried that the British Cabinet Plan denying both freedom and democracy to India may be upset. If the League leaders really wanted an anti-British hartal, they should have approached, not the Governor, for the declaration of public holiday, but the fellow non-League patriots for a joint and powerful demonstration against the British. On the contrary, I have definite information that in certain circles of Calcutta, the idea of coercing the Hindus into a strike on the 16th is being talked about. The result would inevitably be a Hindu-Muslim clash and not an anti-British demonstration".

Basu continued, "It will be the endeavour of our Party to keep peace and unity among workers, with a strike where necessary, and to appeal to both the parties accordingly. We appeal to all not to precipitate any clash between our own brothers, but to make a common stand against the common foe" (League Direct Action Day: Jyoti Basu's Statement, *Amrita Bazar Patrika*, 14 August 1946). This statement is vitally important, as later their activities would show that in practice, their pledge for peace and communal harmony ended up helping the League leadership in unleashing a reign of terror.

The Communists had other compulsions too. The Bengal Premier, who were friendly towards the Communists, had only a month back cancelled the notification by which the following 19 associations (alphabetically arranged) were earlier declared unlawful:

1. Abhoy Ashram, Comilla Town
2. Barkanta Abhoy Ashram, P S: Chandina
3. Kanya Sekhalaya, Birajpur, Comilla Town
4. Khaddar Bhandar, Kandaripur, Comilla Town
5. Kirti Dal, Bengal
6. Mainamati Abhoy Ashram, P S: Burichang
7. The Bengal Jute Workers' Union
8. The Bengal Match Factory Workers' Union
9. The Calcutta Committee of the CPI
10. The Calcutta Communist Party
11. The Calcutta Port and Dock Workers' Union
12. The Chatra Yuva Samsad
13. The City Motor and Transport Workers' Union
14. The Indian Proletarian Revolutionary Party
15. The River Steam Navigation and Indian General Navigation and Railways Companies Labourers and Workers Union

16. The Santosh and Tarakeswar Memorial Committee
17. The Workers' and Peasant's Party (Bengal Chapter)
18. The Workers' Party of India
19. The Youth League, Bengal

As one can see, many of these organisations were related to the CPI, directly and indirectly, and the idea was to keep the Communists in good humour (Ban on Bengal Associations: Bengal Government Cancels, *Advance*, 5 July 1946).

The second favour bestowed upon the CPI was the decision to release all pre-reform political prisoners. This decision was taken on 15 August. Most of these prisoners were of Chittagong Armoury Raid fame, who had later converted to Marxism while serving their prison terms. The CPI found them handy, as after their release, they could be used in campaigning for the party. In the public eye, they were patriots rather than Communists, and the CPI thought that the indoctrination of the masses should be easier by them. The prisoners thus released included:

Ambica Chakravarty
Ananta Singh
Ganesh Ghose
Hem Bakshi (Rangpur Conspiracy Case, Rangpur)
Lalmohan Sen
Loknath Bal
Nalini Das (Cornwallis Street Shooting Case, Calcutta)
Sahairam Das
Subodh Chowdhury
Sukhendu Dastidar
Sunil Chatterjee (Watson Attempt Case, Calcutta)

Calcutta was rife with rumours. No doubt, something sinister was brewing, and when the day of reckoning had almost arrived, on 30 July, the *London Times* commented editorially, 'A Setback in India'. It continued: "It is unworthy of responsible statesmen to indulge in wild talks of gaining their ends by 'direct action' and of abandoning constitutional activities at the moment when their country stands on the threshold of new and decisive developments. The Muslim League would have served the cause of the community far better if it had protested in dignified terms at the provocative tone adopted by certain Congress Party spokesman and had plainly stated that its participation in the Constituent Assembly depended on the observance of the agreed terms of the plan of May 16th except in so far as they might be modified by consent".

On the same day, the President of the Indian League in America, Sardar J J Singh appealed to the United Nations to intervene so that humanity might be safeguarded. The decision of the Muslim League was generally regarded as disappointing and deplorable, much as it had quite possibly caused by a sense of frustration at the League not being called upon to form an Interim Government. It probably feared that the Congress would dominate. Another editorial in the *Hindustan Standard* said, "The air is thick with rumours about the plan of the stalwarts of the Muslim League in the province to make their demonstration a success by coercing the opponents to suspend their normal business for the day. What we desire to emphasise on the present occasion is the very strong and very genuine difference of opinion that exists on the propriety of the observance of the Direct Action Day... of the Muslim League. Nationalists of Bengal, be they Hindus or Muslims, are opposed in principle to the mandate of the League. With them the issue involved is a vital one. They cannot and will not participate in a demonstration the object of which is the repudiation of all their cherished political principles. Millions of such nationalists all over Bengal claim protection from the Government against coercion to which there are likely to be subjected by the overzealous followers of the League" (Responsibility of the Government, *Hindustan Standard*, Editorial, 16 August 1946).

Amrita Bazar Patrika commented, "If the hartal passed off peacefully, the credit would not go to the Muslim League Ministry that had sought to coerce the people into observing it, and that Direct Action Day was a preparation for the forcible establishment of Pakistan. By imposing a general hartal on the public by force, the League Ministry of Bengal wanted to tell the world that all communities were for Pakistan (A Dishonest Move, *Amrita Bazar Patrika* Editorial, 16 August 1946).

Meanwhile, the preparations were complete. After offering their Jumma Prayers, the Muslims from different wards thronged the Maidan. The slogan raised was, "Ladke lenge Pakistan!" The Muslim League Party organ had already urged the Muslims to

> Rise! For the Day is passing
> And you lie dreaming on,
> The others have buckled
> Their armour,
> And forth to the flight
> Are gone.
> Each man has some
> Part to play;
> The past and the future
> Are nothing
> In the face of the stern
> To-day!

(*Morning News*, 16 August 1946)

The foot of the Monument was set as well. Seats had been reserved on the rostrum and within the enclosure and the following were admitted:

Organisers and officials of the Calcutta League

League MLA and MLCs (Bengal and Central)

League Councillors and Aldermen of the Corporation

President, Secretary and Treasurers of the Ward and Branch Leagues under the Calcutta District Muslim League

President and Secretary of Bengal Students' League and Calcutta Students' League

Office bearers of the Jamiat-i-Islam

Office bearers of Anjumans Labour Organisation
Ulemas and Sardars
Honoured guests from other communities
Press (separate seats reserved)
(Direct Action Day Programme, *Morning News*, 16 August 1946)

The man to lead the proceedings was H S Suhrawardy, the Bengal Premier and the mood was tense. The allies also joined the proceedings. S K P Kirchu, President and Ganpat Lal, Secretary, Chotanagpur Jharkhand Scheduled Castes' Federation arrived in Calcutta from Ranchi to specially attend the Direct Action rally. Kirchu was to address the mass rally and invite the leaders of the Bengal League and the Bengal Scheduled Castes' Federation to Jharkhand where the Adivasis (aborigines) and the Scheduled Castes were jointly fighting with the Muslim League for the freedom and Independence of Jharkhand, Pakistan (Mr Kirchu in Calcutta, *Morning News*, 16 August 1946).

The same day, that is on 16 August, Sir Feroz Khan Noon, addressing a huge public meeting held at Mastan Shah Bagh, Bombay, under the auspices of the Bombay Provincial Muslim League and presided over by I I Chundrigar, appealed to Dr Ambedkar and the 6,00,00,000 Harijans of India to embrace Islam and join the Muslim League. Noon described the Congress as a bloc of capitalists, exploiting the working class movements for gaining its own ends. Noon further asserted, "This is another reason why there cannot be any compromise between the Congress and the Muslim League. Islam stands for Socialism. In Pakistan, all the industries will be nationalised and capitalism abolished". He then appealed to the Communist and other anti-capitalist organisations to join hands with the League in its fights against capitalism. Noon advocated Muslim participation in labour movements and strikes (Noon Woos Harijans, Reds and Socialists, *Bombay Chronicle*, 17 August 1946).

This was not for the first time that staunch loyalists like Noon made an ironical appeal to the CPI. In April 1946, Sir Firoz declared that Russia might come to the aid of the Muslims if the British and the Hindus declined to give them an Independent Pakistan. Sir Firoz further said that a population such as Muslims would be entitled to appeal to the United Nations for relief if they failed to get it during the pending negotiations. Noon noted that the Communists were already penetrating into the Muslim ranks in the North West India, and should the Muslims fail to get Pakistan at the end of present negotiations (Cabinet Mission), the Communists would themselves be in a tight spot. Noon even referred to the similarities between Islam and Communism. The two basic differences were of course that Muslims believed in God and private ownership of property but Communists did not. But then both Muslims and Communists favoured the ideology of equal shares, and both sought to stand by the down-trodden! (Noon Banks Upon Communist Aid: Reference to Russia explained, *The Pioneer*, 12 April 1946)

This opinion of Noon might be his personal but it was made from the League platform. The *National Herald* commented that, actually, Noon's intention was to tell Britain that, since the Muslim League enjoyed the Indian Communists' support, the Pakistan movement had the blessings of Soviet Russia and it would, therefore, be a folly on Britain's part, to resist it (Russia and Pakistan, *National Herald*, 11 April 1946).

Coming back to Direct Action on 16 August in Calcutta, the supporters of the two parties – the CPI and the Muslim League – congregated at the foot of the Monument on the Maidan. After offering the Jumma Prayers, Muslims started moving towards the Maidan. The Inspector in Patrol on Russa Road (rechristend as Deshapran Shahmal Road in Tollygunge are) saw at about 13:30 hours, a Muslim League marchers (about 125 persons) were crossing Russa Road from the South towards the North. The marchers carried green and red paper flags mounted on bamboo sticks and iron rods (IB File No. 717(d)/46, Communal Matters, Item 16).

The Bengal Communist Party, under the directive of the Head Quarters, had embarked upon a joint participation with the League on 16 August, and it was not restricted only to Calcutta. At the districts too, both Parties jointly celebrated the Direct Action Day.

Here are some such instances:

HOWRAH: On the night of 12 August 1946, at about 20:00 hours, Mangru Tatoa (CPI), the Secretary of the Bally Jute Mill, moved through the coolie bustee of the Jute Mill and informed both the Hindu and Muslim workers, by beating drums, not to join their work on 16 August 1946 and asked them to observe the Hartal on that day.

On 13 August 1946 at about 17:30 hours Amar Mukherjee and Mangru Tatoa, both of the CPI, called a meeting near the gate of the Jute Mill, in which they also threatened the workers as well as the shop-keepers of Bally Hapta Bazar of facing dire consequences if they did not participate in observing the Direct Action Day. The people of Bally Bazar hearing this news from Hapta Bazar, sent a petition through the office of *Ananda Bazar Patrika* requesting the Bengal Government and local police for interference, as they were apprehending trouble by the Muslim League and the CPI workers.

The IB department noted, "It was clear that the CPI members were trying to make a hold on the Muslim workers of the Mills by co-operating with the Muslim League in observance of the Direct Action Day. Similar activities of the CPI were also noticed in other industrial concerns". This note was signed by Sarat Chandra Sen, DIO (V) Howrah (IB File No. 717/46 (Howrah), Report on Communal Riots resulting from the Direct Action Day, called by Muslim League on 16 August 1946, p.88 and 119).

MIDNAPORE: 'Leaflets were circulated before 16 August, in the district asking Muslims to observe Direct Action Day and urging title holders to renounce their titles ... About 1,000 Muslims paraded the main thoroughfares of Midnapore town shouting the usual League slogans ... A public meeting attended by about 3,000 persons was held with Khan Sahib Kabiruddin in the chair. Ali

Hossain, the local CPI worker and also the Secretary of the Town Muslim League spoke on the perfidy of the Cabinet Mission towards the Muslim League (IB File No. 717/46 (Midnapore), Report on Communal Riots resulting from Direct Action Day, called by Muslim League on 16 August 1946, p.4).

HOOGHLY: On 16 August 1946, in observance of the Direct Action Day as declared by the High Command of the Muslim League, no hartal was observed in Chandernagore. The educational institutions functioned as usual. The local shops including the market opened as usual excepting some shop-keepers who closed their shops under the instigations of the local CPI along with some local Muslim leaguers (IB File No. 717/46 (Hooghly), Report on Communal Riots resulting from Direct Action Day, called by Muslim League on 16 August 1946, p.7).

DACCA: Some three or four days before the Direct Action Day, the local Muslim League Secretary, along with the CPI and the RSPI workers began to preach before the public that the Direct Action Day was a move against the British imperialists and not against the Congress or the Hindus. B Dasgupta, Dacca's Municipal Chairman, later reported the proceedings of 16 August, saying that on the inevitable day, a huge procession with big bamboo lathis in the hands of the participants passed through some of the main thoroughfares of the city and assembled at the meeting in an exclusively Muslim area. The content of the speeches made, soon turned from attacking the Government to the Congress (How 'Action Day' Troubles Started in Dacca: Municipal Chairman's Statement, *Hindustan Standard*, 2 September 1946). The CPI along with the League workers jointly organised a strike and picketing at the four textile mills at Narayangunj and at Hardeo Glass Works at Dacca (Dacca Communist Conduct, *Hindustan Standard*, 1 September 1946).

Within a few days after these reports appeared in the newspapers, Makhan Pal, Secretary, Bengal Provincial Committee of the RSPI sent a letter to the editor, clarifying his party's position. The statement reiterated that no instruction in favour of the participation by the RSPI in the Direct Action Day was issued either from the Central or Provincial Head Quarters of his party. It was further stated that it was not part of the policy of the RSPI to support a reactionary Pakistan demand of the Muslim League or to participate in any kind of direct action by the Muslim League in support of Pakistan although such action might masquerade under the garb of fake anti-Imperialism (RSPI Stand Clarified: *Hindustan Standard*, 3 September 1946). The Communist Party of India, however, refrained from issuing any such clarifications.

BURDWAN: On 16 August printed hand bills in Bengali entitled 16 August Zindabad over the names of Saiyid Ali Hussain, Secretary, Burdwan District Muslim League and other members of the League, were circulated in the town. Almost all Muslim shops in the town observed hartal on this day. Some local CPI workers also moved through the town carrying the CPI flags and organised a rickshaw-pullers strike in sympathy with the demands of the Muslim League. A meeting was held in the afternoon in the Town Hall, under the chairmanship of Dr Abdul Khaleq, Vice-President of the district Muslim League. The speakers explained that Indian Muslims should make a firm stand under Jinnah's leadership against British Imperialism (IB File No. 1138/46, Communal matters/arms (Gen), Use of arms in connection with communal disturbances p.43).

Aftermath: No-Confidence

"Calcutta will be taking many months recovering and many years remembering. Muslims and Hindus that have lived in harmony side by side are, for as long as their living memory lasts, separated and severed from all sympathy. The numbers of the dead have so far been accounted at 4,000 and 15,000 are numbered injured ... The many empty stomachs, together with the filth and garage that have strewn the place, the four-day old corpses on the streets and those that have gone underground to the sewers by way of open manholes – all these coinciding with the return of hot weather to a crowded shattered city make possible, perhaps probable, a plague that will make a pale thing even of the most hideous of holocaust." (City of Corpses – Kim Christen, *Amrita Bazar Patrika*, 24 August 1946)

What happened for four days in the second city of the British Empire was hitherto unprecedented. Even the biggest riot to happen in the city before this, in the twenties, was no match to the damage and scars that Direct Action left on the hearts of the inhabitants of this unfortunate city. For days the streets were littered with unclaimed corpses with scavenger vultures feasting on them. For days there was no sign of Governance. Army came into action when already three days had elapsed. The riot proved that it was a well-thought-out happening. Both sides had made arrangements beforehand, with a boom in the illegal arms market, a gift from the vacated Allied forces of the Second World War. Muslim National Guard and the Hindu Mahasabha workers had made full use of it.

Slowly leaders of all political parties came together with appeals of peace. Rescue and rehabilitation commenced with the corporation workers having their day outs. *Times*, London, commented, "Local leaders of the Muslims as well as of the Hindu communities have toured the city in an endeavour to assuage the fanaticism which has blazed up. But they have discovered that the most eloquent appeals to patriotism and the most conclusive affirmations of the folly of indulging in fratricidal strife when India stands on the threshold of Self-Government are powerless to restrain the orgy of loot, murder, rape and arson, which has swept the city during the last few days. They have discovered, moreover, that the only effective protection for peaceful persons resides in the strong if now overtaxed arms of the police and the military ... It is not difficult to conjecture why Calcutta alone became the scene of so serious an outbreak when similar demonstrations in other places passed off in more or less orderly fashion. Nowhere else in India is the contrast between Hindu wealth and Muslim poverty so glaringly obvious as in the capital of Bengal, a Muslim-majority province whose principal city has become a great Hindu centre of business. In this province, a Muslim League Government is in control of law and order. The Government was not willing to admit sufficiently quickly that good Muslim Leaguers could degenerate into a dangerous mob. Adequate precautions were not taken to protect Hindu life and property in due time, and when the Hindus, driven to desperation, began to hit back the situation passed entirely beyond the control of the civil authorities" (Lessons from Calcutta, *Times*, London, 20 August 1946). *The Statesman*, Calcutta named it, 'The Great Calcutta Killings', much to the discontent of the Muslim Leaguers who threatened to boycott the newspaper.

Bhawani Sen, in his report to P C Joshi, dated 23 August 1946, described the situation in Calcutta, where he admitted that it was the Muslim League that had first provoked the Hindus during its rally. These excerpts show how the riot started:

1. "In the afternoon, there was a huge Muslim rally on the Maidan. Muslim leaders like Suhrawardy and Nazimuddin instead of giving sane counsels fanned the fire in the most irresponsible manner. It was yet within their power to stop the catastrophe if only to save Muslim life but they refused to play that role. They described stories of Hindu obstinacy to the path of Pakistan and urged them to defend the honour of Islam. Abul Hashim, as usual, explained that the target was British but to the listening crowd it was nothing but meaningless phrase. When the meeting was dissolved, the entire crowd went back looting, burning and pillaging Hindu homes and shops on their way."

2. "Up to 16 evening, it was a communal riot of the ordinary type with which every Indian city is familiar. When the night drew closer, it was a dreadful sight. At night, the Hindus began reprisal with Muslims' counter-reprisal. Throughout the night of 16 August and 17 August till mid-day, horrible crimes that were committed on mass scale surpass anything known in the history

of criminology in this country. In this phase, Hindu population in its own *mohulla* combed out all the Muslims and butchered them in most dastardly manner. Similar cruelty was perpetrated in the Muslim *mohullas*...Dead bodies of one's own community were collected and specially exhibited to see that no one hesitates to kill. Kill, Kill, Kill became the slogan in everybody's mouth and everybody tried his best to put this slogan into practice with the thoroughness of a criminal drunkard. The Muslim, the Sikh, the Marwaris, the Bengali Hindu Bhadralok everybody seized with the crime fever."

It was the time for the blame game, once the rescue and rehabilitation started. The Legislative Assembly met in the third week of September and the Congress tabled two motions of No-Confidence, one on the Premier and the other on the entire League ministry, for discussion. Emotions ran high, the motions were fiercely debated – and lost. Kamini Kumar Dutta of the Congress blamed the League demonstration for the riots. Days before 16 August, the Muslim League sponsored press had been persistently poisoning the Muslim minds through writings calculated to influence bitter communal hatred and was openly advocating violence and publishing sinister significance of the Direct Action Day inaugurated in the month of Ramzan. Nagendranath Mahalanobis of the Hindu Mahasabha accused Suhrawardy of having control over the *goondas* of Calcutta, and while he was assuring the House of the neutrality of the administration, his agents fanned far and wide to collect *goondas* from outside Calcutta, while his followers in the city were collecting lathis, daggers, brickbats and other lethal weapons for the Direct Action . . ."

It was Dr Shyama Prasad Mukherjee of the Hindu Mahasabha who challenged the Muslim League in a threatening tone, "My friends (of the League) complain that the Muslim League has been bypassed," he continued, "(but) supposing Mr Jinnah was asked to form the Interim Government without the Congress; what would have happened? Would then the Muslim League blame the Cabinet Mission?" Then he surmised,

"What happened in Calcutta was not the result of a sudden explosion. It was the culmination of an administration, corrupt and communal, which had disfigured the life of this great and happy province...and we say that you shall not get Pakistan! Even if I had belonged to the Muslim League, I would not have minced matters. Whether civil war will gain Pakistan for you is a matter yet to be seen". "Muslims," he continued, "constitute 24 per cent of the Indian population and they say they will never agree to live under Hindu domination. If that is their attitude how can they expect that 45 per cent of the population of this province will ever agree to live under a Constitution where Muslims alone will dominate? If a civil war breaks out throughout India will that help 24-25 per cent Muslims in India against 75 per cent non-Muslims?" He then asked, "Who suffered most during the Calcutta Killings? It is the poor and the innocent. Why should leaders lose their heads and create a situation which they cannot control? We must create a state of affairs which will make it possible for us to build a future of Bengal which will be good for all, irrespective of caste and community" (Riot Debate in Assembly: Shyama Prasad Mukherjee, *Amrita Bazar Patrika*, 21 September 1946).

George Morgan, leader of the European Group clarified, "We are not criticising the Government because it happens to be a Muslim Government. Had any Government been in power, our criticism would have been the same. If failure of maintaining law and order had had similar results as that which in our opinion, brought about the disaster of 16th August to 19th August...This is a question of the failure of the Governance, however constituted, to protect the people committed to their charge. On that score the present Government could not escape criticism".

From the Muslim League benches, the MLAs vehemently defended the position of the Ministry and accused the Hindus, especially the Hindu Mahasabha and Shakti Sanghas for initiating the riot. Hamidul Haq Chaudhuri argued that one of the features of the riots was that organised Hindu educated men started the "cowardly attacks on unarmed Muslims". With the utterance of 'Jai Hind', Azizul Haque complained, the first blow was dealt: so it was preposterous to suggest that the Muslim League started the riots in a city like Calcutta, where the Hindus were in a large majority and so organised. According to W Zaman, what happened during the riots clearly proved that the Congress Hindus were determined that the Muslims would not be allowed even to speak of Pakistan or to get it. And lastly, Abul Hashim, like the Communist he was, blamed the British diplomacy, and gave a call for Hindu-Muslim unity. The motion was lost (Riots Debate, *Amrita Bazar Patrika*, 18 September 1946).

The CPI took a neutral stance. Rajani Palme Dutt, who had by then returned to London, blamed the Cabinet Mission for the Calcutta riots. He declared that the Cabinet Mission had re-introduced communal rivalry, as each party considered it important to score a point, and stake its claim to the Government of India (Dutt Blames Cabinet Mission for Calcutta Riots, *Bombay Chronicle*, 24 August 1946). The General Secretary, P C Joshi, perhaps on the basis of the report received from Bhawani Sen, issued a statement where he said that it was not a matter of argument but was already tragically proved on the streets of Calcutta that the Muslim League's struggle was directly against the Hindus, thus distancing his Party from the responsibility of what had happened (League's Struggle Actually Anti-Hindu: *Amrita Bazar Patrika*, 21 August 1946).

The surprise also came along with it. Even after criticising the 'reactionary leadership' of the League, the CPI ended in helping it by not voting against the League Ministry during the No-confidence motion! Joshi, in a Political Circular, dated 23 August 1946, admitted that, "there are no water-tight compartments between the League masses and the Red Flag masses but as the party can and does influence the mass following of the League, so does the fratricidal policy of the League influence and immobilise the Muslim toilers under the Red Flag" (IB File No. 865/46, Searches of CPI offices in Calcutta and other places on 16 September 1946, Political Circular No. 46/46, 'On Party and the Muslim League,' Item 20, p.31). The main question faced by the Party was how to analyse the Calcutta Carnage without damaging its existing base. In another letter to the Bengal Comrades, written on 27 August 1946, Joshi directed it to change the line of agitation immediately pronouncing that it was the Cabinet Mission Award that set Hindus and Muslims at each other's throats. It was only provoking the Congress and the Muslim Leaguers against each other that the British could hold their sway over the masses. Joshi in his letter admitted that the Muslim League not only bungled but was provocative at the Maidan rally – and was responsible for what happened thereafter. But publicly accusing the League Ministry or voting with the Opposition in the Assembly against the Muslim League Government happened to be tricky.

"We can vote against the Muslim League Ministry PROVIDED IT DOES NOT EFFECT OUR MUSLIM WORKING CLASS BASE (emphasis original) and we can carry it with ourselves through our intensive explanatory campaign . . . If we cannot keep up even our hold on existing organised working-class, everything is lost, even for the future." Thus the best way possible to keep all in good humour was to stay neutral. Joshi continued, "We can also remain neutral and it appears to us here that this is likely to be the best course". On the other hand, voting against the Muslim League had other serious implications. "If we vote against the Muslim League, the disadvantages are not only Section 93 again but also more provocation from the Muslim side". Joshi knew it well that in the then existing charged environment, a call for Coalition Ministry, "is a voice in the wilderness, but since that is the only way out we must stick by it and popularise it . . . Jyoti and other MLAs must speak like inspired beings with self-confidence. All our three MLAs must tour our entire working–class belt and EXPLAIN & Explain" (IB File No. 865/46; Searches of CPI offices in Calcutta and other places on 16 September 1946, Political Circular to Bengal Provincial Committee, 27 August 1946; Item 01). Thus in order to maintain its control over the Muslim workers, the Party decided not to vote against the Ministry but continue criticising the British.

Jyoti Basu issued the following statement, "We Communist members of the Assembly did not rise in support when leave to move a motion of no-confidence against the Council of Ministers was asked for. Our reasons are simple. A one-party Ministry is a standing provocation to civil war, but so are all efforts to overthrow this ministry. The only way out is an All Party Ministry and the way to achieve it is not blaming each other but seeking a common agreement round a table for a common programme that will save Bengal. Calcutta has passed through an unprecedented orgy of mutual slaughter and communal tension throughout the province is acute. To carry the quarrel inside the Assembly after handing over the streets to the military can only worsen the situation. We Communists never help brother fight brother but endeavour to bring them together against the common enemy". Certain questions here, however, remained unanswered. In his statement given on the eve of the Direct Action Day, Basu had stated that he had definite information that at certain places the League workers had forced Hindus to join the Direct Action Day. Was it in return for the favour they received from the League Ministry, or was it their bond with the League? Or was it because they did not want to antagonise the Muslim workers of their unions by opposing the League Programme?

Jyoti Basu, Ratan Lal Brahman and Rupnarayan Roy, the three Communist MLAs maintained their 'neutral' stand during the voting. Participating in the debate, Basu said, in case of a communal riot, they had invariably condemned Imperialism as its main instigator. Their opinion did not vary on the present occasion. He accused the officials of Whitehall, in New Delhi, those of the Governor's House in Calcutta and the members of the British Cabinet delegation for the trouble. In other words, Jyoti Basu blamed just about everybody for the riot – except the Muslim League Ministry. Jyoti Basu did not criticise the non-governance of the League Ministry for the sufferings that Hindus and Muslims together underwent (Riot Debate, *Amrita Bazar Patrika*, 18 September 1946).

The CPI was, however, criticised by both left and right. While Soumyendranath Tagore of the Revolutionary Communist Party of India criticised the CPI joining the reactionary League (Tagore, *Against the Stream, Resurgence of Tribal Savagery in Calcutta*, Vol. II, p.197), Pattabhi Sitaramaiya of the Andhra Congress described the alliance as 'unholy' and warned that such acts would not be tolerated. Even the press was sarcastic. The Editorial of 'Advance' observed, ". . . In the Assembly, the European party, Anglo-Indians, Indian Christians, Communist members and two Scheduled Caste members (Bhola Nath Biswas and Dwarka Nath Baruri) did not rise in support of leave being granted to move the motions . . . The Communist members had, perhaps, become enamoured of the Muslim League because prominent members of the organisation had hinted at their seeking support of Russia – the Mecca of their political pilgrimage" (*Advance*, 24 September, 1946). Similar was the observations of *Hindustan Standard*, "It is curious how self-interests make strange bed-fellows. The Europeans and Communists made a common line-up, though their political ideologies are poles apart. Either you have faith in a Ministry or have not. If the neutrals had faith in the Ministry, why did they trot out that nonsense about the collapse of the administration in Calcutta (this was against the Europeans)? The logical consequence of the speeches of their spokesmen in the Assembly should have been their own vote against the Ministry, which would have buttressed the point they had made – that is a vote in support of the no-confidence motion. But the pangs of conscience of the neutrals had eased after their fiery talks. After all, they are all worldly-wise and could not fail to know which side in the bread is buttered in this province. Why desert the pampered child for the sake of abstract justice sacrificing advantages that are so much more solid!" (Perverted Judgment, *Hindustan Standard*, 22 September, 1946).

Meanwhile, all the pre-reform political prisoners were released by the beginning of September. After their release, they came to Calcutta and met Hashim at his residence. Abdullah Rasool of the CPI introduced Ananta Singh, Ganesh Ghose, Ambica Chakravarty, Lokenath Bal and others to Hashim. They even had lunch at Hashim's house (Hashim, Abul, *In Retrospection*, p.115).

The CPI decided to use these revolutionary-turned-Communists for its own cause. This had a distinct advantage, as in public perception they were brave patriots and the Communists simply wished to utilise their public appeal. These Chittagong convicts now towed with the Party line and started campaigning for Communist policies like Congress-League Unity. In a reception held in Munshigunj, Dacca, on 4 September, Ananta Singh urged the audience to beware of the British policy of divide and rule in India to perpetuate her dependency on England. He said that if the Congress and League were combined and presented a united Front there was no power on earth to retard the freedom of the Indians from alien rule. Samsuddin Ahmed, Secretary, Dacca District Muslim League (and a Communist too) supported Singh and appealed to the Hindus and Muslims to forget the past and fight for the Independence of the country, obviously on the basis of Pakistan. Ananta Singh added that because he was an uncompromising fighter for freedom, he was converted to Communism which, he thought, was the sure guide to freedom (Freedom through Hindu-Muslim Unity, *Ananda Bazar Patrika*, 10 September, 1946).

Later in a press conference held at the residence of Snehangshu Acharya, Singh again expressed the hope that India would soon be free and Majdoor-Kisaan Raj would be established in the country. Sunil Chatterjee, another colleague of Singh, stressed on Congress-League unity for attainment of freedom. In a joint statement by J C Gupta, All Parties Political Prisoners Release Campaign Committee, Lal Mian or Chaudhuri Moazzem Hossain (Muslim League), MLC, also Joint Secretary of the above committee, Prof K P Chattopadhyaya, Habibullah Bahar (League), Muzaffar Ahmed, and Bhupesh Gupta (both from CPI) welcomed the news of the cancellation of the ban on Subhas Bose, while maintaining their differences with Bose (*Ananda Bazar Patrika*, 11 September, 1946).

Along with this line, the ex-Chittagong convicts and other workers of the CPI started criticising the Congress, holding it indirectly responsible for the Direct Action, by joining the Interim Government, a line very much similar to that of the League. The CPI and Muslim League of Chandannagore held a joint reception of the released state prisoners. Har Shankar Mukherjee of Chandannagore Communist Party and Abu Syed of the Muslim League organised the whole affair. In that reception, Ambica Chakravarty urged the people to organise and fight against the British Imperialism under the Red Flag (IB File No. 558/46, Ratan Lal Brahman, p.25). Similarly, the 7th Annual Conference of the Mymensingh Students' Federation was held on 26-27 December 1946, with Ganesh Ghose as President. Prof Abdul Latif Biswas of Islamia College, Calcutta, Prof Satya Ranjan Bhattacharya of Kusthia Town, Annada Shankar Bhattacharya, Secretary, Bengal Provincial Students' Federation and Shamsuddin Ahmed, Secretary, Dacca Muslim League also attended the proceedings.

Shamsuddin blamed the British for communal rioting and supported the Tebhaga Movement. Ganesh Ghosh deprecated the acceptance of office in the Interim Government by Nehru, who, he said, had become a pawn in the hands of the British (IB File No. 501/45, Annada Shankar Bhattacharya, Extract Folder II, p.385).

This stance of lending indirect support to the League continued. The Party continued to criticise the 'reactionary leadership' of the League but could not sever their relationship with it. Even after Direct Action the criticism continued. The Bengal Provincial Communist Party held the League responsible for failing to protect the lives and properties of the citizens. It went to the extent of saying that the Government had not made a single honest effort to bring the two communities together but instead had allowed the military and the police to harass and persecute the innocents (Failure to Protect Lives and Property of People, Communist Criticise Bengal Government, *The Pioneer*, 9 November 1946). The Communists did not, however, organise any form of agitation against the Muslim League Government.

The Party perhaps had certain considerations. Just a few days before the Direct Action, the Muslim League members in the UP Assembly tabled three amendments to the official resolutions viz. on the abolition of all kinds of capitalism such as private ownership in land, industry, mines, banking, insurance, and also nationalisation of principal means of production, exchange and distribution (Abolition of Capitalism, 3 Amendments by League Party, *National Herald*, 13 August 1946). In September, Yusuf Abdulla Haroon of Sind Muslim League tabled a resolution before the Sind Provincial Muslim League Council for the appointment of a delegation by the Muslim League to proceed to Moscow to secure Russian support to their cause. He even went to Paris and met M Molotov, the Soviet Foreign Minister (Haroon to Meet Molotov, Pak through Soviet Aid, *National Herald*, 25 September 1946). The results of their talks were not disclosed; but, *Bombay Chronicle* inferred this as the reason for the Communist supporting the League in their Direct Action programme (Proof At Last: Attitudes and Latitudes, *Bombay Chronicle*, 7 September 1946). Thus the Communists carried on with their lip-service, attacking the League, but not altogether distancing itself from the League. This continued even during the Noakhali mayhem, when P C Joshi appealed to the 'progressives' of the League to bestir themselves and take a hand in resisting the reactionary elements in the League. Joshi went to the extent of describing Noakhali as another Calcutta in the countryside, equally gruesome and revolting. Even the Communists were not spared, as their party office in Chittagong was attacked and workers stabbed, 'in the very presence of the District Magistrate' (All Party Mission to Noakhali: Joshi's Suggestion, *Amrita Bazar Patrika*, 21 October 1946).

Although it was clear that the Party had joined the League Programme in order to keep their Muslim workers in good humour, yet there was no intention of the Party to join in rioting is a suspect. The Hindu party workers of Keshoram Cotton Mills at Lichibagan, Metiabruz were butchered by the League fanatics. A letter dated 24 August 1946, written by some Hindu and Muslim workers of the Communist Party, Metiabruz, addressed to P C Joshi, reached the Party Headquarters at Bombay. Here the writers expressed their dissatisfaction against Syed Abdullah Farooqui, the leader of the local Communist Party. Here are some excerpts: "Comrade Farooqui has not only taken an active part in instigating the Muslims against the Hindus, he has also openly associated himself with the Muslim hooligans who slaughtered anything between 500 to 800 people of the locality."

During the Great Killings "Farooqui was found moving in the cars of the local League leaders, in which League Flags were prominently hoisted". The writers then appealed the top leadership to take adequate action against Farooqui as they had no faith in Dr Ranen Sen, who supervises the Party in that area, as he ". . . is hopelessly ignorant of the detailed activities and there is no hope that a weakling like him who always is commanded by Farooqui instead of commanding him and who always depends upon the mercy of the latter for his own popularity" (IB File No. 717/46, Communal Riots after Direct Action Day, observed by Muslim League, SL No. 279 & IB File No. 772/41 of S A Farroqui, Extracts, p.55). Such statements of different Hindu Oriyas criticising the role of Farooqui, beginning with Saturday 17 August, was sent to the Provincial Committee of the Party. Curiously, the Party, instead of taking action against Farooqui, tried shielding him! Adhikari sent a copy of the letter sent to them to Bhawani Sen, requesting him to take necessary precautions to 'protect Comrade Farooqui, who is slandered here' (IB File No. 717/46 (24 Parganas) & IB File No. 772/41 of S A Farroqui, Extracts, Communal Riots after Direct Action Day, observed by Muslim League, SL No. 279, p.56). The Bengal Party enquired about the Farooqui incident and praised Farooqui for his effort to maintain peace and decried those who made anti-Communist propaganda (IB File No. 772/41 of S A Farroqui, p.118).

Meanwhile, some workers of the Cotton Mill lodged a formal complaint against Farooqui. Farooqui was arrested by Metiabruz Police in connection with the PS Case No. 9d/25 August 1946 u/s 148/380/436 IPC with 9(80, 21(8), 19(8), 17(8), 23(8), 13(8), 14(8) and 4(9). He was named by the following workers of the Keshoram Cotton Mills and boarders of Elias Buildings who were victims of 17 August 1946 massacre: Fagu Das, Dwarikanath Bera, Chintamoni Bhuiyan and R Das. All the workers were then living in the Mill compound. They testified that Farooqui was present at the time of the mass massacre in Elias Buildings, Metiabruz. Farooqui was seen with Elian Mistry ordering the mob to loot and murder the Hindus. This report was made by the DIB, 24 Parganas, Alipore, 17 August 1946 (IB File No. 279, 717/46 (24 Parganas), Communal Riots after Direct Action Day, observed by Muslim League, copy of DIO Report 17August 1946, p.53). The charge-sheet filed against Farooqui was (a) that Farooqui tried to instigate communal rioting, (b) he along with certain Muslim Leaguers gave false assurance to 300 Oriya Hindu labourers, and finally (c) when these labourers were attacked, Farooqui and his colleagues simply looked on.

Farooqui was the President of Garden Reach Textile Workers' Union. Madhab Munshi, Secretary of the Union issued a press statement saying that the charges against Farooqui were entirely false and without any foundation (Hindu Press Lie Nailed, *Morning News*, 6 September 1946). Farooqui was released on bail and subsequently acquitted altogether. He later became member of the Organising Committee of the Calcutta District Committee of the CPI, the working Committee of the PBPTUC and the General Council of the AITUC and MLA on CPI ticket.

As for the followers of Ambedkar, twelve persons had accompanied Jogen Mondal to the Maidan. In the riot that followed, according to figures provided by Ramananda Das, Secretary, Bengal Provincial Depressed Classes' League, more than 1,000 Scheduled Caste Hindus, mostly muchis, dosads, doms, methers, dhobis and others lost their lives. Besides, 40,000 muchis in various parts of Calcutta were robbed and looted. Some of the followers of Mondal, who joined the League procession on 16 August were spared because they wore Muslim League badges (Riots and Ambedhkarites, Letter from Ramananda Das, Secretary, Bengal Provincial Depressed Classes' League, *Amrita Bazar Patrika*, 28 September 1946). But as a reward to his loyalty towards League, Jogen Mondal found a berth in the Interim Government as a League candidate!

It may be a good idea at this point to refer to a debate in *The Statesman*, Calcutta. One Habibur Rahman, claiming to be a Radical Humanist, and Hatim Khan wrote letters to the Editor with the view that the Great Calcutta Killing was a class conflict between the haves and have-nots, and was, basically, economic in nature. The overwhelming majority of Hindus in Bengal represented the haves (capitalists and the middle-class) and the Muslims, have-nots (agriculturalists and industrial workers). The upper class Hindus wanted to perpetuate their economic domination and the oppressed, the Muslims and the Scheduled Castes tried to get out of that trap. The result was the gruesome riots. The writers then urged all progressive forces in India – Communists, Radical Democrats, Socialists and others to join hands and strengthen the League. Along with this, they clarified that though the Muslim League was not a progressive or a Leftist Party, it had unconsciously played a progressive and revolutionary role. Stating his view, one O P Dubey from Delhi opined that the unholy alliance of the Communist with the League was a sad comment on the practice of Communism and Socialism and perhaps the best illustration of political opportunism. 'Leftist ought to know that in the event of transfer of power in consequence of a British understanding with the Leftist-League coalition, it will be the League that will get the upper hand because of its huge mass following, secured by sentimental appeals of Islam and Pakistan. The regime thus established will not be socialist but communal.' Another contributor, S K Sengupta, reminded that the theory of League 'unconsciously playing a revolutionary and progressive role was similar to what many German Social-Democrats preached about Nazi movement in its younger days. How they and the workers they had led paid was in history (Economic Basis of Communalism/Letter to the Editor by Habibur Rahman and Hatim Khan, *The Statesman*, 7 September 1946; O P Dubey and S K Sengupta's reply, 24 September 1946).

The Muslim League missed a great opportunity in establishing itself as an alternative platform of anti-imperialist expression. With other marginalised parties, they had succeeded in grouping together; they could have provided an alternative leadership. But they failed dismally because they were not in the habit of taking a full-fledged anti-Imperialist stance, being ardent loyalists most of the times in their history, who had seldom gone into clashes with the Government. By the very nature of the call given by the League, it was bound to turn into a struggle against the Congress and the Hindus. The 'Progressives' inside the League were not in a position to counter the emotional upsurge initiated by the hardliners. On the other hand, the Hindus had also made arrangements to counter any provocations.

CHAPTER TEN

United Bengal

It began on the streets of Calcutta, wandered to the countryside of Noakhali, crossed borders and entered Bihar, then to the countryside of Punjab, via Gar-Mukteswar. A spectre of communal orgy and blood-bath, indeed, civil war, loomed large on the destiny of 'Akhand Hindustan'. By the end of 1946, the two chief contending parties, even after joining the Interim Government could not agree on the administrative issues. Home went to the Sardar Patel of Gujerat, while Finance went to the Nawabzada of Punjab. And gradually it became clear that the two could not meet at a common point. The alternative was to part, but the question was, how? By then the concept of Pakistan had crystallised, but its final shape was yet unknown. The leaders threatened, howled or remained silent. Meanwhile, street fights continued.

After the carnage at Noakhali and its subsequent repercussions in Bihar, chances of a civil war were imminent where Calcutta and Noakhali had given the Hindutva-brigade an issue to kick-start their hate-campaign. Similarly Calcutta and Bihar were also being used by the Muslim communalists in the League and its para-military outfit, the Muslim National Guard. Newer organisations such as Anti-Pakistan Front started becoming vocal. This particular Front was organised by a Chitpavan Brahmin by the name of Dattatreya Laxman Patwardhana in 1943. Patwardhana was once a member of the Working Committee of the All India Hindu Mahasabha. After his death in 1943, L G Thatte took over the position of the General Secretary of the Front. In a letter dated 12 November 1946, addressed to The President of the Bengal Hindu Mahasabha, Thatte expressed that, "atrocities on Bihari Muslims were the natural consequence of atrocities on Bengali Hindus". He then praised the Bihari brothers for they had shown that they shall not tolerate any brutalities either in Noakhali or in Tipperah (IB File No. 1416/43, Anti-Pakistan Front, p.9). He sent a letter to the editor of the *Amrita Bazar Patrika* on 12 September 1946, making it clear that, "I know that Jinnah is dreaming that Hindus will be cowed down to accept Pakistan within a short time. But let me be frank enough to tell Mr Jinnah and his colleagues that Pakistan or Muslim Raj in India is impossibility in the future. We Hindus are no longer of that type which the ancestors of Jinnah (not in fact but as Mr Jinnah wants them to be) were fortunate enough to have during the last 1,000 years. We have learnt much from our Muslim brethrens and we are now in a position to teach them how to behave with Hindus. To be brief, we will prefer KABARSTHAN (emphasis original) of both the Hindus and Muslims to accepting Pakistan or Muslim rule in India (IB File No. 1416/43, Anti-Pakistan Front, p.5).

By the end of 1946, a formation called Bengal Partition League, with such men like Hemanta Kumar Sarkar, Nalinakshya Sanyal, Major A C Chatterjee (INA), Jadav Panja, Shyama Prasad Mukherjee, Upendra Nath Bannerjee (Editor, *Basumati*), Dr Sisir Kumar Banerjee, Subodh Chandra Mitra, Sailendra Kumar Ghosh, among others, had been formed. Their demand was to divide Bengal with the reason given was the tyrannical rule of the Muslim League Ministry which posed a direct threat to the Bengali culture and public life, and to the general well-being of its citizens. The evidences were the Calcutta Killings and the genocide at Noakhali, but at the same time they kept mum on the retaliation of the Hindus in Calcutta and Bihar. This association was later rechristend as Bengal Provincial Conference with their demands remaining the same.

Shyama Parasad Mukherjee of the Hindu Mahasabha eventually emerged as the leader with brotherly indulgence from Sardar Patel. In a letter written to Kanji Dwarkadas, in March 1947, Sardar had observed that if the League insisted on Pakistan, the only alternative was to divide Bengal and Punjab. The League could not have the whole of Punjab and Bengal without a civil war. Patel even hoped that, "a strong centre with the whole of India, except, Eastern Bengal and a part of Punjab, Sind and Baluchistan, enjoying full autonomy under the centre, will be so powerful that the remaining portions will eventually come in". Later events, however, proved him wrong.

Shyama Prasad Mukherjee, much as he belonged to the Hindu Mahasabha, was close to the Sardar by temperament. He argued that if Bengal's constitution was left to be determined by a body of persons, the majority of whom were dominated by the policies of the Muslim League, whether in or outside the Indian Union, no protection could be expected from their hands. Thus the demand for a separate province was large enough in area and population wherein more than two-third of the total Bengali Hindus could reside. But the natural question was what would be the future of the Hindus in East Bengal? To Shyama Prasad, the creation of a Hindu Bengal, linked up with a strong and representative Indian Union, "will be a source of tremendous strength in saving the minority Hindus in East Bengal". Shyama Prasad was thinking of a hostage situation when he pointed out that, "In Hindu Bengal, there will be about 60 lakh Muslims. No Muslim Government functioning in East Bengal would easily like to torture and torment the minority Hindus in as much as it would be anxious in its own interest, to ensure the minority Muslims in Hindu Bengal should receive a fair and equitable treatment at the hands of the majority representatives" (S P Mukherjee's Analysis, *Amrita Bazar Patrika*, 20 March 1947). This hypothesis too, did not come true.

Meanwhile, the Bengal Provincial Congress Committee prepared a draft resolution asking the Muslim League to forthwith

1) Abjure the so-called Pakistan scheme at least so far as it relates to Bengal

2) Accept joint electorates with reservation of seats, for the time being in the legislatures and other elective bodies in the Province on the basis of adult population of the respective communities

3) Direct all its adherents to return to their relatives, all abducted
    women, and stop further criminal activities of the kind
    perpetrated in Calcutta, Noakhali, Tippera, Bogra and other
    places
4) Pending execution of the above programme, forthwith
    reconstitute the Bengal Cabinet with equal number of members
    from both the major communities with Premiership going to
    a Congress man for the interim period and
5) Should signify its reactions to the foregoing within a fortnight
    at the latest, meanwhile abandoning and suspending all legislative
    measures designated to assist in establishing Pakistan in Bengal.

The BPCC warned that notwithstanding the above offer to the Muslim
League, a broad based campaign should be initiated immediately to
prepare the ground for effecting the separation of the Hindu majority
areas of Bengal from the rest should the Muslim League reject the
foregoing, and that an appropriate committee of Action be formed
on that behalf (IB File No. 1128/46(i), SL 459, Bengal Partition League,
p.165). So it became clear that the Congress was also thinking in terms
of Partition.

The man opposing this demand for Partition was Sarat Chandra
Bose. Bose argued that any question of Partition would seriously affect
the interest and position of the Hindus. Scheduled Caste Hindus who
formed a predominantly large percentage of the Hindus in East Bengal,
in case of Partition, would be directly affected as the well-to-do section
would naturally be inclined to move out of East and North Bengal to
migrate to West Bengal. This would leave the poorer section of the
caste Hindus and Scheduled Caste Hindus to their fate in an area which
would be converted to Pakistan. Bose then attacked the Hostage Plan
and exclaimed how one Provincial Government could give any effective
protection to the Minority community living under another provincial
Government. Sarat Bose then demanded:

•   When power is transferred, it must be transferred to an Indian
    Union of which the Province of Bengal shall be a unit.

- There must not be transfer of power separately to the divided portions of India.

Sarat Bose found allies in Akhil Chandra Dutta, Naresh Chandra Sengupta, Tulsi Ch Goswami, Leela Roy, Surendranath Biswas, Purna Das, Amiya Chakravarty and Kiran Shankar Roy, among others (Bengal Partition Opposed, *Amrita Bazar Patrika*, 25 March 1947). The Caste-Hindu society of Bengal was thus clearly divided with the former depending more on emotion and threat perception, which, to a large extent, was true.

The solution to the Bengal problem, provided by Sarat Bose was a United Sovereign Bengal, chiefly, based upon emotional grounds of Bengali sub-nationalism. Bengal was to become an Independent Sovereign Nation, with joint electorate, where power would be shared by both the communities. Surprisingly, Bose got two Muslim Leaguers as allies to his United Bengal scheme: Abul Hashim and Suhrawardy!

Abul Hashim, with his own interpretation of Indian History, always maintained that there was no such thing as an Akhand Hindustan, a concept similar to the Communist theory of Nationality. Very much like the Communist, he based his supposition of Pakistan on this theory. Explaining the Pakistan scheme in a meeting at Rangpur, 1945, Hashim said that India was the home of many nations and had never united in the past except by political and military pressure from outside. He was of the view that one precondition for the League to fight for freedom of India was the assurance that India would be divided into a number of autonomous sovereign states on territorial and linguistic basis (The Pakistan Scheme Explained, *Star of India*, 2 February 1945). This was also the view of the Communist. He reiterated his position again during 1946 Elections.

Hashim could place his theory on the basis of the Pakistan Resolution with the demand for independent state existence of 'contiguous units' where Muslims were in majority. The United Bengal was one such unit with Muslims in majority. He argued the Hindus and Muslims agree to the 50:50 formula of C R Das, and even declared that in the free state of Bengal, Hindus and Muslims, "shall have no right exclusively reserved for them except the right of Muslims to govern their society according to their own Shariat and the rights of the Hindus to govern their own society according to their Shastras". Thus, it gave the Muslims their spiritual need for Pakistan and the Hindus a real homeland for free development of their ideology and material realisation of their particular outlook in life (United Bengal Remedy for All Present Ills: Hashim, *Star of India*, 30 April 1947).

Such declarations were confusing and full of ambiguity as it did not provide a concrete solution to the communal problem. The official League later did not approve the C R Das formula and vehemently attacked Hashim, although their Quaid-e-Azam was exactly demanding the same 'parity' at the centre!

Hashim came in touch with Sarat Bose to jointly work for attainment of United Bengal. Their secret meetings came to the notice of the CPI through Shamsuddin Ahmed of the Dacca Muslim League who was a Communist and had accompanied Hashim in such rendezvous. The Communists gladly published this 'breaking news' in their Bengali organ, 'Swadhinata' causing much discomfort to their former fellow traveller. Hashim immediately issued a rejoinder denying such meetings and attacked the Communists, accusing them of spreading rumours to create disruption amongst Muslims and the Muslim League. He even said that the Communists' call for League-Congress unity was a ploy to build up their own party over the bones of the Congress and the League (Communist After Creating Disruption Among League Leaders: Hashim's Stern Warning, *Morning News*, 28 January 1947). This coming from the biggest 'progressive' in the Bengal League was kind of a set-back to the Communists.

H S Suhrawardy, the Bengal Premier, was the other gentleman to support Bose. For Suhrawardy, it was a tactical move as he knew that in Pakistan his hegemony on Bengal would surely dwindle. Just days before the Direct Action, he had threatened saying Bengal shall be declared an Independent State if the Congress was put into power (Independent Parallel Government in Bengal: Suhrawardy, *Hindustan Standard*, 11

August 1947). Similar declaration was made by M H Gazdar, the President of Sind Muslim League. To Suhrawardy, Independent Bengal was an alternative plan to retain his supremacy over Bengal politics, a trump card of sorts, as perceived by him. In answer to whether the United Bengal would later be linked up to Pakistan, whether he would accept Joint Electorates, whether the scheme had the blessings of Jinnah, Suhrawardy refrained from giving any answer. When asked whether he feared the other provinces and the princely states to take up the same attitude and become independent units on the basis of linguistic and cultural homogeneity and if so whether he envisaged a federation or confederation of such units, he answered, "I am only concerned with Bengal. You cannot impose a federation from the top. What is really needed is basic autonomous States that will be free to choose their destiny. Then you can have a real federation where each unit voluntarily gives up some rights on their own for the benefit of the federation" (Mr Suhrawardy's Plea for United Bengal, *Star of India*, 28 April 1947). Suhrawardy's plan was more than just a United Bengal. He had even advocated a separate sovereign state under Adivasi control to be framed out of the districts in which the adivasis predominated – Singhbhum, Manbhum, and Hazaribagh way back in April 1946 (Mr Suhrawardy on Status of Pakistan Unity, *Hindustan Standard*, 3 April 1946).

Suhrawardy, who had all along demanded a separate homeland for the oppressed Muslim nation all these years, controlled the Direct Action Day proceedings, suddenly became the champion of common culture of the Bengalis! But such common ties existed between the Hindus and Muslims of other Provinces as well, nullifying the very basis of Pakistan demand. Thus the posture taken by the architects of 16 August carnage was perceived as an opportunist move by the Hindu community. In fact, after the Great Calcutta Killings and Noakhali Genocide, Suhrawardy had become enemy number 1 in the eyes of the Hindus. His advocacy of a United Bengal only strengthened the demand for Partition. Nalini Ranjan Sarkar articulated the public mood when he expressed surprise at Suhrawardy's belated discovery of ties of blood and cultural affinities among the people of Bengal – both Hindus and

Muslims. Until then, promoting the League's Pakistan demand, he had always denied any such cultural affinity (No Alternative: Nalini Ranjan Sarkar, *Amrita Bazar Patrika*, 20 April 1947).

Sardar Patel, keeping track of the developments in Bengal, was of similar opinion. In a letter to Surendranath Sen, retired judge, on 1 June 1947, he pointed out, ". . . people in Bengal have seen through the whole game and it is not likely that except for a few selfish individuals anybody will be taken in by the propaganda that is being carried on in the pompous name of a 'Sovereign Bengal'. The League people are now glibly talking of one race, one culture and one language; till yesterday they were swearing to their being a different nation, having a different language and a different culture. Nobody will fall into this trap in Bengal".

In another letter to K C Neogy, Sardar Patel had described the United Bengal scheme as a trap in which Sarat Bose and Kiran Shankar Roy may fall, and that the only way to save the Hindus of Bengal was to insist on Partition. Shyama Prasad Mukherjee described the scheme as a virtual Pakistan (Surendra Mohan Ghose, *Amrita Bazar Patrika*, 1 May 1947).

A similar situation had also developed in Punjab, with incessant violence between the communities. The League had demanded fresh elections and claimed Punjab as an integral part of Pakistan. Sardar Kapur Singh, Deputy Speaker of Punjab Assembly commented that even if League won all Muslim seats, it could not run a Government without the support of the minorities. After the kind of violence partly initiated by the Muslim League, the minorities could not agree upon a United Punjab. To them United Punjab meant Pakistan and the minorities were not to submit to it. Either the League gave up the Pakistan demand or it agreed to Partition Punjab (United Punjab Meant Pakistan: Sardar Kapur Singh, Deputy Speaker, Punjab Assembly, *The Tribune*, 7 April 1947). The situation in Punjab was to deteriorate very fast.

It would be wrong to assume that this demand for dividing Bengal was totally based on communal grounds. The threat, especially after the Calcutta Riots, that persisted and the genocide at Noakhali, even after Gandhiji's epic tour, convinced many a rational mind that Partition was inevitable. Vested interest was surely there, but it mingled with the threat perception (See: Chatterjee, Joya, *Bengal Divided*). Thus we see the civil society of Bengal, men like Sir Jadunath Sarkar, Dr Megnad Saha, Dr Sisir Mitra, Dr Suniti Kumar Chatterjee, among others sending appeals to Sir Stafford Cripps and Sir John Anderson, former Governor of Bengal, for the formation of a separate West Bengal Province guaranteeing the safety of life and unhindered progress in education, industry and commerce under a non-communal Ministry. Ten thousand telegrams were sent to the Viceroy Lord Mountbatten demanding Partition of Bengal (*The Tribune*, 14 May 1947). *Amrita Bazar Patrika* conducted an opinion poll wherein 98.3 per cent of voters supported the move for Partitioning Bengal. Tushar Kanti Ghosh, who then owned *Amrita Bazar Patrika*, was one of the chief architects of this demand for Partition.

Non-communal political organisations were also divided on the demand for Partition. Prominent Forward Bloc leaders like Hemanta Kumar Bose, Amar Bose, Haridas Ghose, Dr Bhupal Bose sent a memorandum to Sardar Sardul Singh Cavesher, President, All India Forward Bloc, stating that although they believed in the linguistic, cultural and fundamental unity of Bengal, it was their considered opinion that in the event of a division of India, there will be an overwhelming demand of the minority community of Bengal for the constitution of a new province in Bengal to remain within the all India Union. Even on the party level, they argued, it would be easier for them to propagate their socialist ideas more effectively within the new province under the Indian Union (Forward Bloc Motion on Partition Disapproved, *National Herald*, 8 May 1947). This memorandum was, however, declined by the central leadership of the Block; by June 1947, this agitation for Partition had, however, picked up a different momentum.

The Scheduled Castes' Federation vehemently opposed any move to divide Bengal as it would surely affect their political position. Jogen Mondal said that the scheme of Partitioning Bengal was only to crush the Scheduled Castes and concentrate all power in the hands of the Caste-Hindus. The Caste-Hindus in East Bengal were mostly rich and influential, so they could easily move from East Bengal to West Bengal while the Scheduled Castes being awfully poor and lived by cultivation of land or catching fish in rivers of East Bengal. By no means could such poor helpless people be rehabilitated in West Bengal. Thus a United Bengal was a necessity in the interest of the Scheduled Castes (Demand for United Bengal: Mondal, *Star of India*, 14 May 1947). Similarly, Deb Narayan Raj, Secretary, Scheduled Castes Chamber of Commerce, expressed great surprise on the demand for Partition of Bengal. Raj broached the theory as a 'conspiracy' of the caste-Hindus. "When the caste-Hindus find themselves in hapless minority – Muslims and Scheduled Castes having joined hands together – some new device for preserving their vested interests was quite natural and this they have forged out…The Scheduled Caste people's only chance lies in keeping company with those who are also the have-nots (Muslims). Therefore, we declare most emphatically that the Scheduled Caste people do not want division of Bengal. They shall work for Greater Bengal" (Partition Not To Be Tolerated, *Star of India*, 21 April 1947).

Dr Ambedkar was in a bargaining mood. If the Hindus wanted Partition, he asked, they would have to satisfy the Scheduled Castes of the following:

i. Where will the boundary line be drawn?

ii. What protection are the Hindus prepared to offer to the Schedule Castes under the new constitution as against what the Muslim League would be ready to offer?

iii. Will there be provision for the exchange of population?

iv. What provision are the Hindus prepared to make for the economic rehabilitation of the Scheduled Castes who as a result of division will be left within the Muslim zone and who will have been brought over to the Hindu zone as a result of exchange of population?

(Ambedkar's View on Bengal and Punjab Partition, *Star of India*, 28 April 1947)

There was a division within the *Depressed Class* as well. On one side stood Mandal with his Scheduled Castes' Federation with the blessings of the Muslim League. On the other extreme point, Radhanath Das emerged as the leader in the Depressed Caste's League with support from the Congress and stood for the merger of the Harijans into Hindu society. Das's League had even Hindu Mahasabha's support in some districts like Mymensingh (IB File No. 191/46, Extract from File 1164-44 General Note, Scheduled Castes' Federation, Part II). Mandal initiated a joint anti-Partition Movement with Muslim League. On 4 February 1947, at Faridpur a meeting was held under the auspices of Scheduled Castes' Federation and the Muslim League, with Dwarikanath Barori in the chair. Members of the Scheduled Castes were advised to work in cooperation with the Muslim League until the Congress felt the weight of their unity (IB File No. 191/46, Extract from File 1164-44 General Note, Scheduled Castes' Federation, p.65). Similarly, Kanai Lal Biswas, member of the Working Committee of the Federation sent a letter to the Secretary, Nadia District Muslim League, dated 8 May 1947, requesting him to furnish names of at least 4-5 Scheduled Caste workers in each Police Station in order to form Scheduled Caste opinion in favour of Bengal anti-Partition movement (IB File 191/46, Extract from File 1164-44 General Note, Scheduled Castes' Federation, p.63).

The CPI's stand on the Bengal situation had changed from time to time. In their original thesis on Nationality, 'Pakistan and National Unity,' Gangadhar Adhikari had stated that, "In case of the Bengali Muslims of the eastern and northern districts of Bengal, where they form an overwhelming majority, they may themselves form an autonomous region in the state of Bengal or may form a separate state," which in a roundabout way meant, Partition! Mind you, this was written way back in 1942 (Adhikari, Ganagadhar, *Pakistan and National Unity*, p.19). In the same thesis, the author, indeed, contradicted himself, when he acknowledged the fact that there were common grounds amongst the Hindus and Muslims in Bengal. But still, Eastern Bengal being a Muslim majority area enjoyed the right of self-determination! This was, in fact, the fallacy of the thesis; on one hand, identifying Bengal as a separate unit and at the same time demanding a separate state existence for East Bengali Muslims! Dr Adhikari writes, ". . . the Bengalis form a distinct nationality and so should be given the right of self-determination. There is much more in common between the Bengali Hindus and the Bengali Muslims than between a Bengali Muslim and say, a Pathan. . . . Eastern Bengal forms a special problem. Here generally speaking, there is a Muslim population of more than 60%. Within the framework of a common nationality, the Muslim peasantry of Eastern Bengal has a distinct cultural entity of its own... We have to recognise this. In the case of nationalities, too, there are such things as transitional forms, and we have to recognise in East Bengal precisely such a transitional phase of development" (*Ibid*, p.46).

P C Joshi too looked upon East Bengal as a separate entity. In an article, Joshi had referred to Muslim people as "Eastern Bengali Muslims" within that category. Some of his comrades even campaigned in East Bengal on that theory of two nationalities in Bengal. Later Bhupesh Gupta sought clarification, ". . . If the East Bengalis had then demanded a separate, sovereign state, our Marxism as applied to national problem, would have seen nothing politically wrong there in terms of fundamental rights . . .This I refer only to stress that we had invented two peoples in Bengal . . ." We then asked, "When Bengalis split into two separate peoples in Marxist eyes, did it still remain a question of emphasis or it became something else? Wasn't Stalin's definition of Nation given a go-by in respect of our basic understanding of the national problem in Bengal?" (IB File No. 865/46, Note for discussion by Bhupesh Gupta, 27 May 1946, extended meeting of the Provincial Committee, from Searches of CPI offices in Calcutta and other places on 16 September 1946, p.337)

In reality, Joshi had a different plan for Bengal. In 1944, he had stated that an Independent Bengal would be established not by plebiscite but with Congress-League Agreement (Overstreet/Windmiller, *Communism in India*, p.496). Finally, the Communists had settled their position on the Bengal situation in line with their Election Manifesto, 1946: "The CPI stands for a united and free Bengal in a free India. Bengal as the common homeland of the Bengali Hindus and Muslims should be free to exercise its right of self-determination through a Sovereign Constituent Assembly based on Adult Franchise and to define its relation with the rest of India" (A Free and Happy India: *Election Manifesto*, 1946).

In the process, United Bengal Scheme of Bose-Hashim-Suhrawardy found quick support from the Communists. The Bengal Provincial Committee of the CPI welcoming the committee that was formed in April 1947 with Sarat Bose as President and Kamini Kumar Dutta as Secretary to resist Partition of Bengal assured that the Communists would follow the policy of friendly co-operation with the anti-Partition committee. Bhawani Sen was of the opinion that the demand of Partitioning Bengal in order to safeguard Hindu interest could not bring unity in India, but would only instigate the Muslims in their demand of Pakistan, culminating into communal fracas. The only way out was United Bengal (Partition of Bengal: CPI Against Movement, *Amrita Bazar Patrika*, 28 April 1947).

The Party had all these years supported Pakistan's demand, so their volte face against the Partition seemed hollow. All the important party members of Bengal were asked to investigate the Partition agitation, viz. signature campaign, mass meetings, group meetings, summary of speeches; the district parties were also advised to send (a) as many joint statements as possible against Partition, (b) as many reports as possible of the meetings and group meetings held against Partition (with details of people participating etc), (c) articles, poems etc. written against

Partition (d) letters to Editor from the Kishans, students, and working class, and left elements against Partition (IB File No. 1128/46(i), Bengal Partition League, Sl. 459, p.206).

While realising its inability to launch an actual direct action in this regard, the CPI, however, tried to establish close contact with other left parties viz. Forward Bloc, RSPI, for a joint front, but that did not materialise (IB File No. 1077/46, Monthly Review of Communist Affairs in Bengal dated 10 June 1947, Compiled from the Reports of the CIO, Calcutta, the DIG, IB, Bengal and the DCSB, Calcutta, p.112). Having failed to bring the other Left Parties to its fold, the CPI resorted to their old practice of infiltrating in the ranks of Forward Bloc, RSPI, and the Socialist Party of India. The CPI already had agents in the League, now they tried to get into the Muslim National Guards, the paramilitary outfit of the Muslim League by professing that the Party as a whole was opposed to the Partition of Bengal. By then the honeymoon with the League was, however, over (*Ibid*, p.81).

The concept of United Bengal had its own demerits – it did not provide any tangible solution to the communal question. For one thing, it already had indications of becoming a subsidiary subaltern Pakistan, much to the abhorrence of the 46 per cent Hindus in the province. The Scheduled Castes' Federation had to support this scheme to maintain its position of being the sole representative of the Scheduled Castes, even after winning just one seat in the Bengal Legislative Assembly. The CPI, too, had nothing to lose. In the event of United Bengal, the Party's proximity with the Muslim League would enable them to join a Ministry. On the other hand, in case of a divided Bengal, they would find enough room to emerge as the principal opposition.

The CPI had always had strong ties with the League. People like Khwaja Nazimuddin and Sir Feroz Khan Noon spoke their language: the League was the party of workers and peasants while the Congress represented the capitalists! In the Madras Assembly on 11 February 1947, while the European members voted solidly with the Congress Ministry, the Muslim League supported the CPI-sponsored resolution seeking immediate withdrawal of the Public Safety Ordinance. Prakasam, the

Congress Premier, expressed surprise at the stand taken by the League (Communist Motion Defeated, *Times of India*, 12 February 1947).

Lastly, Syed Abdullah Brelvi, the Editor of the 'Bombay Chronicle', had this to say about the changed policy of the CPI: ". . . My Communist friends who always ridiculed me for my sentimental 'petite-bourgeois' faith in the Unity of India and hostility for the ideology of Pakistan, who were ready to divide India into two or twenty pieces in pursuance of their theory of self-determination, have suddenly become fanatical believers in the Unity of India!" (The Last Page by Chronicler, *Bombay Chronicle Weekly*, 1 June 1947)

Brelvi went on to say that, "I think a change has been rung in the Party line over Pakistan. I sensed it coming when a shrewd and seasoned Communist like R P Dutt (privately of course) expressed sharp differences with the CPI on this very issue. He thought the Indian Communists had gone TOO FAR (emphasis in original) in placating the reactionary feudal League and in supporting Pakistan which, he said WAS NOT the same as the Soviet self-determination. . . . If they have really come to see the error in their previous pro-Pakistan policy, I am only too glad . . . instead of indulging in ideological sophistries to wriggle out of the contradiction, the Indian Communists should publicly admit that they had committed a grievous blunder in supporting the League demand for Pakistan which has led to the vivisection of the country and the triumph of imperialist diplomacy" (The Last Page by Chronicler, *Bombay Chronicle Weekly*, 29 June 1947).

In lending its support to 'United Bengal,' the Party indirectly supported the League. In case of a divided Bengal or Punjab, the Muslim League had no usefulness, and thus the League all along wanted the whole of Punjab and Bengal. Jinnah knew that he had to bargain hard for attaining his cherished dream. As early as in February 1946, Jinnah, through the honourable Aga Khan, had sent a message to the Viceroy, Lord Wavell, that he was willing to part with Amritsar, Ambala etc. in the North-West and the Hindu districts of Bengal and Assam but not Calcutta (Moon, Penderel (Ed.), *Cabinet Mission: Opening Discussions Wavell: The Viceroy's Journal*, p.215).

Sir Feroz Khan Noon demanded a homeland for the 84 lakhs Muslims in the UP having cultural ties with Delhi and Aligarh with spiritual loyalties to Ajmer, which would be federated with Pakistan (Homeland for UP Muslims: Mr Noon's Solution, *Times of India*, 9 May 1947). Likewise, Abdul Rahman, Chairman of the Reception Committee of the 5th Mysore State Muslim League, held at Shimoga, in April 1947, demanded Mysore be developed into an Independent Sovereign State (Mysore Should Be Independent, *Times of India*, 18 April 1947).

M A Warsi, Secretary, Division of Bihar Conference, demanded the Partition of Bihar into Hindu and non-Hindu autonomous provinces, and supported the Adivasi demand for a separate state of Jharkhand initiated by the Adivasi Mahasabha (Partition of Bihar, *Searchlight*, 5 May 1947). The Council of the Madras Presidency Muslim League passed a resolution demanding a separate state of Moplastan on the west coast consisting of large areas of Malabar, South Kanara and the Lakshadeep Islands which were predominantly occupied by the Muslims (Madras Muslim League Demands Moplastan, *Morning News*, 3 June 1947).

The Agra Muslim League passed a resolution at a public meeting held in the Jumma Masjid stated that Agra should be included in Pakistan, because it has been the oldest Muslim Capital of India (Demand of Inclusion of Agra in Pakistan, *Morning News*, 4 June 1947). Dr Emran Hussain Chaudhury, MLA, Member, Committee of Action, Provincial Muslim League, demanded the inclusion of Assam into Pakistan, stating that the League had the support of 3 lakh Ahoms, 19 lakh tea garden labourers, 7 lakh Scheduled Castes and 16 lakh tribals (Congress Invited to Visit Mankachar 'Killa', *Morning News*, 4 June 1947).

S M Rizivanullah, Secretary, Muslim League in the UP Assembly demanded five Muslim states inside India as under:

1) Districts of Saharanpur, Moradabad and Bijnor, and the tehsils of Mujaffarnagar, Jansath, Meerut
2) Mauna in the north-west UP
3) Districts of Lucknow, Sitapur, Sandila and Hardoi tehsils, UP
4) Purnea district of Bihar which is contiguous to Bengal

5) Districts of Santhal Parganas, Rahe Muslim State in Malabar consisting of the whole district except Khattyam and Palghat

These five states were to be sovereign, but part of the Pakistan State. "The argument advanced in favour of the division of Punjab and Bengal was that non-Muslims of the East Punjab and the West Bengalis should be given the option to go out of the Muslim zones and join up with the Hindu majority zones. May I ask if the same argument would be accepted in case of the Muslims and other non-Hindus who did not agree with the ideology of the Mahatma-ridden Congress?" questioned the UP League leader (UP Leader Demands 5 Muslim States in Hindustan, *Morning News*, 4 June 4 1947).

The Communist Nationality theory came handy for the Leaguers. Now the grand old Communist's in the UP League, Hasrat Mohaani, entered the arena with his 'scientific' demands. At a conference, held under the auspices of the Sind Muslim League in May 1947, a resolution supporting the demand for Akhand Pakistan and protesting against the proposal of Partitioning Punjab and Bengal was passed, with Mohaani being the Chairman. The resolution suggested a Union of Indian Socialist Republic, on the Soviet model of Sind, Punjab, Bengal, Assam and the NWFP. The conference also welcomed the proposal for convening at an early date, a convention of all those elements of political thoughts in India who were opposed to the Partition and who advocated the establishment of a Union of Indian Socialist Republic on the lines of the Soviet Union in order to counteract the move of the Congress to establish a unitary dominion of Akhand Hindustan (Akhand Pakistan on Soviet Model: Sind Leaders demand, *Times of India*, 8 May 1947).

Meanwhile, in Trichinapoly, on 16 June 1947, S Muthiah Mudaliar demanded the establishment of an Independent Sovereign State of 'Dravidistan' consisting of Tamil, Telegu, Malayalam and Karanese speaking areas of Madras Province (Dravidistan, *Searchlight*, 18 June 1947). Apparently these demands might look baseless and just a mere ploy to put pressure on the Government. But a closer look would point to the basic fallacy of the Pakistan Resolution, 1940. All these demands were raised from the Provinces where the Muslims were in minority, who had fought equally, if not with much more vigour, for the attainment of the Promised Land. In fact, the schools of Deoband and the Aligarh Muslim University, the nerve-centres, were the breeding grounds of the students whose contribution to the movement was immense. Tragically, these areas were to be severed since in the original Lahore Declaration, the demand was for Independent Nations for those units wherein the Muslims were in a majority.

On the other hand, the Congress-sponsored Harijan League, at their 15th Annual Session under Hem Chandra Naskar, passed a resolution declaring that the Harijans in India were with the Congress and that they were not prepared to accept Pakistan, Achhutstan or Sikhistan (Indian Annual Register: Jan-June, 1947). P R Thakur, MLA and Scheduled Caste Member of the Bengal Assembly stated that the Partition of Bengal was a settled fact and appealed to the Scheduled Castes living in East Bengal not to be unnecessarily perturbed about their fate in Pakistan (*Searchlight*, 3 May 1947). This posture was diametrically opposite to that of the followers of Ambedkar in the Province.

The Bengal Muslim League launched a vigorous campaign against the Partition agitation, asserting that Muslims in Bengal were determined to maintain the integrity of Bengal at all cost and shall not yield an inch of her territory. 'Pakistan will not be a day's purchase if through sophistry and blackmail, large chunks are torn away from it.' (Cutting the Nose: *Morning News*, 10 April 1947) The League even tried to whip up Bengali sentiments by accusing centre for all its woes. Fazlul Rahman, the Minister of Land, commented, "The Hindu leaders are fully aware of the step-motherly treatment which Bengal has hitherto received at the hands of the Central Government. While other Provinces have developed their commerce, education and industries at the cost of Bengal with the help of the Centre, we have remained where we were, in spite of all our resources. Bengalis had always been neglected and treated as alien by the Central Government. Thus the duty of Bengalis, both Hindus and Muslims, was to sever all relations with the Centre and progress as citizens of Independent Bengal (Bengal Partition Merely a Political Stunt, *Star of India*, 8 April 1947). But this did not help much.

At the same time, the League used the clerics to add religious overtones to their demands. Anti-Partition resolutions were passed at various mosques in Lahore, expressing their extreme indignation against the move of Partitioning Punjab and Bengal (Anti-Partition Resolution Passed in Lahore Mosques, *Morning News*, 6 May 1947). The Bengal Muslim League, initially taken aback by the stance taken by their two foremost leaders for the cause of a United Bengal, came out to reiterate its loyalty to the All India Muslim League and its policies. Akram Khan, Habibullah Bahar took the lead to criticise Hashim's diabolic attempts at the 50:50 formula. Akram Khan clarified the League's ideal was the establishment of a sovereign Muslim Nation comprising the six units of Punjab, Sind, the NWFP, Baluchistan, Bengal and Assam, and there was no question of a separate Independent Bengal isolated from Pakistan. Khan stated that Muslim India constituted a single United Nation and those who were talking of a Bengali Nation consisting of Muslims and Hindus were playing into the hands of the enemies who proposed to 'sandwich' Muslim Bengal between the Hindu Provinces in the east and in the west. Khan even dismissed the 50:50 formula as undemocratic (Muslim Bengal Wedded to Pakistan: Akram Khan, President, BPML, *Morning News*, 5 May 1947).

In the midst of all this confusion, Humayun Kabir came out with an interesting idea. Pointing out that the division of Bengal was just as meaningless and harmful as the division of India, Kabir asked Suhrawardy to retrieve his position and justify the racial unity of all Bengalis and that of United Bengal, by passing a bill, or at least, a resolution, accepting joint electorates of the Province and inviting the Congress Party in the Bengal Legislature to join the Cabinet on the basis of equality. "There should be joint responsibility," Kabir pointed out, "which, in the particular case of Bengal entails, that if the Legislature expressed want of confidence even in one member of the Cabinet, the whole Cabinet should go and the member of the outgoing Cabinet should be ineligible for inclusion in the Cabinet to be formed" (How to save Bengal? Prof Kabir suggests, *The Tribune*, 12 May 1947).

It was a positive idea, but nothing of that kind was expected from Suhrawardy, thus further strengthening the demand of the Bengali Hindus. Akram Khan, on the other hand, decoded a 'conspiracy theory' of the Hindus between the lines of Sarat Bose's United Bengal Scheme. He found the formula to be a conspiracy to bury the aspirations of 30 million Muslims of Bengal and the rising Scheduled Caste movement and perpetuate them to a state of serfdom. According to Khan, the Caste-Hindu plan was somehow to break the League Ministry, so that they could have full control over the administration at the time of the transfer of power. The demand for joint electorate was seen as a ploy to dominate the Muslims and the Scheduled Castes. It was impractical as the Scheduled Castes were demanding separate electorates and their rights in the present position of backwardness could not be challenged. Caste-Hindus with their superior financial, educational and political status had the power to interfere. Thus *Joint Electorate* was, to Akram Khan, a negation of democracy (Akram Khan Exposes Sarat Bose's plan, *Star of India*, 14 May 1947). The threat-propaganda of the 'others' prevailed in the attitude of both the sides.

The United Bengal Scheme hit the rock-bottom. The Hindus would not have it: and they demanded Partition; the Muslims could not think of sharing power with the Hindus and they demanded the whole of Bengal. The final efforts were made by the propagators of the scheme by trying to take Gandhi into their fold. Gandhi's queries to both Suhrawardy and Hashim were simple: whether they would object joining Pakistan, if Pakistan wanted them to enter in a 'Voluntary Federation' for the propagation of Islamic Culture and Religion? Whether Sovereign Bengal contemplated entering into a voluntary association with the rest of India, having regard to the fact that Bengal's common culture had its roots in the common heritage not only of Bengal, but the whole of India, actually no fruitful answer came from the champions of United Bengal (See Pyarelal, *Gandhi: The Last Phase*, Vol. II).

Further, the top Congress leadership was not in favour of any idea of a separate existence of Bengal. Nehru and Patel saw the United Bengal as a design to divide Hindus and indirectly connecting the whole of Bengal with Pakistan, with its 45 per cent Hindus as perpetual minorities. The Congress, perhaps, was also aware of the fact that in the event of a United Bengal, they would not be able to form a Ministry in the near future.

In June 1947, Lord Mountbatten announced his Award. Bengal and Punjab were to be divided. Both Congress and the Muslim League discussed the Award and it could not be said that their decisions were unanimous. The AICC accepted Partition by 157 to 29 votes, with 32 members abstaining from voting. It accepted the Partition of India as the alternative to Balkanisation and chaos. The principal opponents were Purushottam Das Tandon, Swami Shahjanand, Ansar Harwani among others. Muslim League, too, accepted its 'Moth-eaten' Pakistan.

The Communist Party's stand on the Mountbatten Award was quite ambiguous. On the one hand, the Party accused the British Government saying that the Mountbatten Award did not give India real Independence but was making concessions to the national demand to transfer of power. At the same time, the CPI thought that new opportunities for national advancement had been won. The two popular Governments and Constituent Assemblies were the strategic weapons in the hands of the national leadership. The CPI, however, stuck to its theory of Nationalities suggesting that the recognition of the right of national self-determination and the immediate implementation of fundamental democratic measures to undermine communal separatism and to preserve and strengthen Indian Unity on the basis of the unity and equality of every nationality. In India, the party was to strive for the abolition of Princedom, for joint electorates, national self-determination on the basis of linguistically demarcated provinces, regional or local autonomy with full democratic rights for the Hill, Frontier and other compact tribal areas. It demanded full protection to the religious and cultural rights of the Muslims, as some Hindus regarded the Muslims as aliens in the Indian Union.

In Pakistan too the Party demanded a Constitution based on adult franchise, joint electorates and proportional representations, and full protection of religious and cultural minorities and national self-determination in the Pakistan Union to ensure equalities of Sindhis, Baluchis, Pathans, Punjabis and Bengalis.

The other Left Parties were opposed to the very idea of Partition. The Forward Bloc, for instance, described the AICC acceptance of Partition as 'Greatest Act of betrayal' (*Searchlight*, 19 June 1947). Even the CPGB condemned the Two Nation Plan (*Searchlight*, 20 June 1947). The Communists in India, although criticised the Partition and campaigned for a United Bengal, actually ended up voting in favour of Partition in the Bengal Assembly! "It has been instructed to remove all suspicion and distrust even by publically admitting its blunder in evolving the policy it had done in 1942, vis-à-vis the People's War" (IB File No. 1077/46, Monthly Review of Communist Affairs in Bengal, dated 10 July 1947, Note on the margin of the sheet, signed dated 12 July 1947, p.119, and dated 10 June 1947, Note on the margin of the sheet, signed dated 25 June 1947, p.112). In a statement issued by Jyoti Basu, Ratan Lal Brahman and Rupnarayan Roy, the Party's stand regarding Partition was clarified: "The Mountbatten Award has left no scope for Bengal to assert her own right of sovereignty, and deciding by her own people's free vote which Constituent Assembly to join, which alone could be the basis for the assertion of the right of self-determination by the Bengali people as a whole . . . The Mountbatten Award with its clear-cut division of the country, having already been accepted by our two great organisations, the Congress and the Muslim League, the Partition is already a reality. In the prevailing circumstances, the demand of the League majority in the Bengal Assembly for the inclusion of the whole of Bengal inside Pakistan can with justice be regarded as an act of coercion, by the Non-Muslim majority in West Bengal. We, therefore, shall vote for the Partition (Communist to Vote Partition, *Amrita Bazar Patrika*, 20 June 1947).

The decision to divide Bengal in order to remain attached to the Indian Union was taken by the Bengal Assembly. Members representing the Hindu majority areas voted for Partition at the Assembly House on 20 June 1947. 58 members voted for Partition and 21 members against it. Jyoti Basu and Ratan Lal Brahman, the two Communists, falling in this area, voted for the Partition. The Muslim League members voted solidly not to join the existing Assembly, while Congress and the Oppositions including the Anglo-Indians voted for joining it. The Communists in this case remained neutral! In the Muslim majority areas, 106 members voted against Partition, while 35 were for it. Communist Rupnarayan Roy voted for the Partition! Thus the Members of the last undivided Bengal Assembly performed his historic role to divide Bengal, which had been, till yesterday, one. The two great communities of Bengal, kith and kin, which had lived together through the centuries, parted company.

Abul Hashim, the valiant Knight of United Bengal, admitted that he had failed to forge all like-minded forces together to save Bengal from the catastrophe. He had even failed in the Muslim League Council, wherein he had tried to justify the call of a United Bengal, quoting from the Pakistan Resolution, where the demand for Independent States where Muslims were in a majority had been made. Jinnah dismissed the whole matter by saying that it was a printing mistake! (Hashim, Abul, *In Retrospection*). Hashim attacked the League leadership saying that he was not given a chance to speak and that the acceptance of the British Plan by the All India Muslim League Council was due more to fear and helplessness rather than satisfaction and hope.

Hashim was depressed because Bengal was not given a chance to choose her own Independent status, the choice being restricted to India and Pakistan. In such circumstances, the Independent Bengal scheme was doomed to failure. It could be achieved if the Hindus of West Bengal opted for Pakistan or the Muslims of the East cast their lot with Indians. Hashim then appealed to all progressive Muslims to form parties on a political socio-economic programme based on the fundamentals of their culture which in terms of modern thought could be called democratic polity, human equality and socialist economy. The guiding principle, according to Hashim, was, 'Keep to the Left' (Hashim Accuses League

High Command, *Morning News*, 16 June 1947). This sparked sharp criticism from the old guards, advising Hashim to mind his own business, that Islam follows the 'Golden Middle Course'. Some even warned Muslim Bengal to avoid Hashim as a plague (Letter to the Editor by one Abdur Rahim, *Morning News*, 17 June 1947). The party organ, 'Dawn' described Hashim as a 'snake in the grass,' a fifth-columnist and advised him to join the Congress (Abul Hashim's Actions Criticised by Dawn, *Morning News*, 18 June 1947).

Both the Congress and the Muslim League accepted Partition as 'something is better than nothing' theory. The Congress and other nationalist forces even had pre-conceptions that ultimately the Pakistani territories would not be able to survive on its own and join the Indian union. The Communist Party soon expelled Joshi and re-grouped under BTR (B T Ranadive) with the slogan, "Yeh Azadi Jhuta Hai". Even after Independence, they would continue for some time to keep contacts with their erstwhile allies. Under Ranadive, with the call of insurrection, the party resorted to Guerilla tactics. West Bengal was divided into zones with leaders who would call for an uprising to violently overthrow the Congress Government. The Calcutta zone fell under Mohd Ismail. Towards the end of June 1949, Ismail participated in a secret meeting of the party at Park Circus, Calcutta, wherein the party leaders were asked to take immediate steps for an armed preparation by collecting bombs, acid bulbs, fire-arms, etc. In about December 1949, he met one Gaffur Ansari at Serampur and asked him to organise the Muslim League members who were still left in Calcutta and to train them up in arms so they might work for the CPI [IB File No. Part II, KW 655/36 File 655(x)/36, History Sheet of Mohd Ismail, son of the late Mohd Khan of Rajputana, Kanpur, UP and 41, Zakaria Street and also of 249 Bow Bazar Street, Calcutta (3rd Floor)].

Epilogue

What did the Communists gain by supporting the Muslim League – that is, by upholding League's two-nation theory? What impact had it on the political outcome that degenerated into the Partition, following large-scale bloodshed? These are the questions that crop up from the discussions above.

There may be three reasons why they did so:

1) The Communist Party of India blindly followed the Soviet Model of the Nationality Theory and, probably, erred in analysing the Indian situation

2) The Communist Party was fully aware of the Indian situation and was supporting the League in order to gain support of Muslim toilers – particularly industrial wage-earners, seamen and peasantry, in other words, wangle the Muslim working class and peasants

3) The Communist Party of India followed the Soviet model of Nationality theory propagated at the time of revolution.

In case of the theory of Nationalities, when applied to the Indian situation, had a number of shortcomings. India was a land of multiple ethnicity, religion, language, etc. It is indeed a sub-continent, where people from different backgrounds, over the centuries, had co-existed. So the separation would not only put an end to it, but would belie past history. India could be split on the basis of language, caste, race, ethnicity, religion and so on. But against the split, the only thing needed was some political consciousness: the awareness that it would be impossible to live apart. On the other hand, the Nationalists, although recognising these differences, were trying to forge a grand coalition, an experiment hitherto unknown to the West, but based on liberal thoughts and democracy. Actually, the idea of one-nation was a matter of perception. Stress was given on the unity in the middle of diversity.

Was there no common bond, no understanding between the inhabitants of this land? There certainly was. There were the great Epics, the Ramayana and the Mahabharata, that held all Indians in thrall, and were part of local cultures. Then there were the great reform movements, the Bhakti and the Sufi tradition, of which preachers had travelled long to spread their cults. It was not surprising to see a Bengali singing Mira Bai's Bhajans, who belonged to Rajasthan. Then there were the religious meeting-points; Prayag or Ajmer Sharif, where thousands from across the sub-continent congregated. There were the great Empires, Maurya, Gupta, Mughal. On top of it all, there were inter-racial marriages, where naturally people would not like their families to break up. These were all psychological attachments that had evolved over the ages.

With the East India Company's rule, and later of the HMG, of which the binding factor was English. Much as it began with the well-to-do, it soon percolated to the commoners: there was some trickle-down effect at least. The English-educated people could read books and then pass the information on to the commoners. Naturally, they came to read about the Western conception of Nationalism. The Hindus were the first to go in for Western Education, and thus they were exposed to new ideas from the West. Thus, quite contrary to the Macaulay's intentions, there rose a class of English-educated Indians, who began to criticise the British Raj. Nationalism had to be 'anti' something and the very presence of the Union Jack fulfilled that need. All the gifts from the ruler – Railways, Telegraphs, Congress – transformed into tools of Nationalist aspirations. It began with petition and soon turned into violent agitation and finally, into a mass movement. The emotional attachments were strengthened through the writings and songs of statesmen and poets of the day. The idea of India had started taking shape.

Rajendra Prasad, the first President of independent India made an interesting observation in this regard. He said, "All Nationalities of India have been the subject of the same central power which is a foreign power. The problem that arises here is not of safeguarding the rights of nationalities *inter se* but against the common central power which equally dominates each and all such nationalities" (Prasad, Rajendra, *India Divided*, p.374). The common enemy was the Union Jack which was perceived as the fountain-head of all evils in India. It was not the question of an 'advanced' nationality like the Bengalis dominating any relatively lesser known ethnic group. All were in the receiving end.

There were, however, inner contradictions as well – for example, the caste-system of Hindu society. Tagore for one had forewarned his countrymen that "those of us in India who have come under the delusion that mere political freedom will make us free have accepted their lessons from the West as the gospel truth and lost their faith in humanity. We must remember whatever weakness we cherish in our society will become the source of danger in politics" (Tagore, Rabindranath, *Nationalism*, p.71). This was evident in the subsequent rise of communal Muslim politics and caste-based politics. The Hindu society, to a great extent, was to be blamed as it failed to eliminate the caste-Hindu mentality with regard to Muslims and *Harijan*s. But these were social problems, as identified by Tagore, which reflected on the political arena much to the comfort of the rulers.

Tagore dreamt of such an India where the provinces would hang together, and the 'where the mind is without fear', and, being Indians, all Bengalees would love 'Golden Bengal' because it is part of India. These two ideas, apparently contradictory, would co-exist. People would take pride in their being Punjabi, Marathi or Bengali, while at the same time, take greater pride in being Indians. India was to be a mosaic pattern, a melting-pot, a noble experiment, till then unheard of in the West. Tagore laid stress on that emotional attachment and noted, "The whole world has become what India has been. The whole world is becoming one country through scientific facility. And the moment is arriving when you must also find a basis of unity which is not political. If India can offer to the world her solution, it will be a contribution to humanity. There is only one history – the history of man. All national histories are merely chapters in the larger one. And we are content in India to suffer for such a great cause" (*Ibid*, p.59). This idea was echoed by Nehru in his autobiography, when he quoted from Sir Frederick Whythe's 'The future of East and West'. Sir Frederick wrote, the greatest of all the contradictions in India, was "diversity making for unity", which was not immediately evident because it failed historically to find expression in any political cohesion to make the country one, but which was so great a reality, and so powerful, that even Islam in India had transformed itself up to a point. To Nehru, *Bharat Mata* was the anthropomorphic form to a country. And for the first time in her history, one India was to get a political shape once she broke the chains imposed upon her by the British (Nehru, Jawaharlal, *An Autobiography*, p.447).

Let us now examine the hypothesis of the third possibility. After the revolution, the Soviet policy started changing. Lenin, for instance, wrote on the Finnish issue, "We stand for giving Finland complete liberty; that will increase their confidence in Russian democracy, and when they are given the right to secede they will not do so. We are for the fraternal union of all Nations...If the Ukranians see that we have a Soviet republic, they will not break away. But if we retain the Milyukov republic, they will break away" (Shaheen, Samad, *The Communist theory of National Self Determination*, p.140). And again, "If we assumed power, we would at once recognise the right of separation of Finland, the Ukraine, Armenia, and of any other nationality which had been oppressed by Tsarism. But, we, on our part, do not at all wish for this separation. We want the largest possible state, the closest possible Union, the largest possible number of nations all of which are closely associated with Great Russians; we desire this in the interest of socialism and democracy" (*Collected Works of Lenin*, Vol.XXI, 2nd Russian Edition, Moscow, 1931, p.316).

After the October Revolution, the seizure of power by the Bolshevists hastened the movement for national independence in the Ukraine, and soon after, in Transcaucasia, which in turn, broke into Georgia, Azerbaijan, and Armenia in the spring of 1918. The new Bolshevik Government in Petrograd quickly recognised the Independence of the Ukrainian People's Republic, with its capital in Kiev, but it showed its real policy in the question of national self-determination by promptly setting up a rival Soviet Ukrainian Government in Kharkov. In the three years of struggle, Kiev changed hands no less than thirteen times! The history of Georgian Independence was somewhat similar, till, finally, in February 1921, Soviet forces entered into its territory to join hands with a 'pro-Soviet' uprising and Georgia was proclaimed a Soviet republic, thus losing its political Independence (Shaheen, Samad, *The Communist Theory of National Self Determination*, p.146).

In China, speaking at the 2nd Chinese National Congress of Workers and Peasants, 23 January 1934, Mao Tse Tung categorically pointed out that the Soviets were decisively against the exploitation of the minorities by imperialism and KMT. Mao promised that, "China recognises the complete self-determination of the minorities who may go so far as to secede and form independent free states . . ." and that, "the free Union of nationalities will replace national oppression" (*Selected Works of Mao*, Vol VI, India 1990, p.90-92). But the reality was something different. Zhou En Lai, in August 1957, put forward his thesis on the National Question. He described China as a "Unitary Multi-National" state and the right of self-determination as conceived by the Russians could not be applied in China (Questions Relating to Our Policies Towards China's Nationalities, Selected Works of Zhou En Lai, Vol II, Peking 1989, p.253-278) Thus, what happened to Tibet was not surprising.

There is another reason why the Communists were supportive of Pakistan: this one is propounded by the political analysts of the day. Maybe, this is hypothetical, but fascinating, nevertheless. Political analysts view that Communists' support to creating Pakistan was part of a bigger international plan.

India and China were the most important countries, when they became free, in South Asia. The resources of these two countries enabled them, at a given opportunity, to become a global power and play a prominent role in the world organisation. This, certain political observers surmised, as an eyesore of the USSR, as it would not suit her at all to have one or two big powerful neighbours in the South Asia. A big country like India or China could not be persuaded against her will to become a sphere of influence, but on the contrary, would insist on being a world power.

The emergence of a strong India, or China was, therefore, not at all conducive to the Soviet expansionist plans. China was then in the midst of Communist-Nationalist confrontation. In India, Pakistan could provide the best means for penetrating into India's body politic. It would be a small and weak state, thus could be easily influenced by Soviet penetration policy. Pakistan had Karachi, one of the finest harbours on the whole Persian Coast. With the Russian dominance in Iran, Pakistan could not remain insensible to Soviet influence. The Communist policy of 17 autonomous units was a design to weaken the sub-continent so that the Congress would become weak, and other influences, like the Communists could become relevant.

This analysis, at least in the chaotic atmosphere of 1946-47, had some grain of reason. Although later developments proved it wrong. The Communists, soon under a new leadership of B T Ranadive, would launch a full-fledged attack on the Indian Nation. It would be the days when the drums of revolution shall beat loud!

Index